THE
UNIVERSITY
AND
REVOLUTION

Edited by

Gary R. Weaver

and

James H. Weaver

 Prentice-Hall, Inc., *Englewood Cliffs, N.J.*

Prentice-Hall International, Inc. (*London*)
Prentice-Hall of Australia, Pty. Ltd. (*Sydney*)
Prentice-Hall of Canada, Ltd. (*Toronto*)
Prentice-Hall of India Private Limited (*New Delhi*)
Prentice-Hall of Japan, Inc. (*Tokyo*)

1739857

We gratefully acknowledge permission to use the brief quotations reprinted in this book from the following sources:

Norman Cousins, "The Crusades for Law and Order," *Saturday Review* (July 6, 1968), p. 16. Copyright © 1968 by Saturday Review, Inc. Reprinted by permission of the publisher.

Robert M. Hutchins, *The Learning Society* (New York: Frederick A. Praeger, Inc., 1968), p. viii. Reprinted by permission of the publisher.

Malcolm X, *The Autobiography of Malcolm X* (New York: Grove Press, Inc., 1966; London: Hutchinson Publishing Group Ltd), p. 341. Copyright © 1964 by Alex Haley and Malcolm X; copyright © 1965 by Alex Haley and Betty Shabazz. Reprinted by permission of the publishers.

Eldridge Cleaver, *Soul on Ice* (New York: McGraw-Hill Book Company, 1968; London: Jonathan Cape Ltd), p. 341. Reprinted by permission of the publishers.

Dick Gregory, *The Shadow That Scares Me* (New York: Doubleday & Company, Inc., 1968), p. 89. Reprinted by permission of the publisher and International Famous Agency, Inc.

John Hersey. *The Algiers Motel Incident* (New York: Alfred A. Knopf, Inc., 1968), p. 298. Reprinted by permission of the author and the publisher.

Robert F. Kennedy, *To Seek a Newer World* (New York: Doubleday & Company, Inc., 1967; London: Michael Joseph Ltd), p. 1. Reprinted by permission of the publishers.

Crisis at Columbia [The Cox Commission Report] (New York: Random House, Inc., 1968), p. 92. Reprinted by permission of the publisher.

Noam Chomsky, *American Power and the New Mandarins* (New York:

CONTENTS

ACKNOWLEDGMENTS

The primary source of encouragement and inspiration for this volume came from the students of The American University. They created the course The University and Revolution and, through the Kennedy Political Union of the Student Association, allowed us to finance many of the lectures published in this text. All royalties justifiably will be turned over to the students to finance other academic projects of this sort which they choose to initiate.

The administration also granted us funds to finance this course and allowed us the freedom to offer this rather unorthodox subject to the students for course credit. They defended us when criticism came and at no point discouraged us from inviting some of the most controversial speakers on the contemporary American scene.

The faculty at The American University who volunteered their help in moderating seminar sessions, counseling students, and reading research papers deserve the major credit for making the course a success.

Our contributors cannot be thanked enough. Many came for honoraria embarrassingly small for their contributions; some refused to accept a fee. All have allowed their royalty fees to be given to the Student Association of The American University.

Lastly, we wish to thank those individuals who helped prepare manuscripts, type, edit, and perform the mundane duties so necessary for compiling these chapters: Ann Ansary, Mike Dixon, Kelby Fletcher, Maurie Goldberg, Jerry Haar, Petie Kahn, and Bonnie Willette.

G. R. W.
J. H. W.

PREFACE

In the spring of 1968, The American University followed the pattern of campuses around the world as it went through a student uprising. The revolt was touched off by the arrest of approximately a dozen students for possession of marijuana. There was evidence that university administrators had not only cooperated in the arrests, but had given out information which led to the arrests. Thus arose the issues of "safeguard of personal privacy and access to student files."

Students and a few faculty members protested the procedures which led to the arrests and submitted a list of twelve demands to the university administration. These demands ranged from "immediate cessation of curfew regulations" to a student "voice in all policies regarding all academic action, faculty assignment, and dismissal." After a week of negotiation between faculty, students, and administration, all but one demand was met through compromise, although as of this writing their implementation has yet to be fully accomplished on the campus. This revolt was a rather peaceful and productive happening which won the praise of Washington newspapers, Congress, and the *Saturday Review*. Norman Cousins wrote:

> It is unfortunate that Columbia University, where relations broke down, should dominate the headlines, while almost no attention is being paid to campuses such as American University, in Washington, D.C., where student protest has been imaginatively and responsibly met and where a pattern of strong student-faculty-administration cooperation is being worked out.*

During this revolution I was an Instructor and Assistant Dean in

* Norman Cousins, "The Crusade for Law and Order," *Saturday Review* (July 6, 1968), p. 16.

the School of International Service at The American University and a resident advisor in one of the men's dormitories. Thus nearly all of my time was spent with students, many of whom were actively involved in this protest. A group of students who had spent a great deal of time discussing civil disturbances, the Vietnam war, education, and the student movement sought the creation of a course where they could study these problems and relate them to their individual interests. Consequently, Dr. James H. Weaver and I agreed to create a reading course: The University and Revolution.

A brief description of the course is included at the back of this collection, along with a bibliography of some of the sources used. Our broad purpose was to assess the impact of the university on the revolutionary movements sweeping the world today, as well as the impact of the revolutionary movement on the university. Most students received pass-fail grades on independent research papers while some fulfilled their course requirement in more creative ways, including oral presentations and even artwork. We tried to allow those students who initiated the course the freedom to structure or "unstructure" it according to their individual needs and interests. Most importantly, however, we stressed dialogue on both the small-session level and the large-lecture level, with guests as diverse as Eldridge Cleaver and Mark Rudd to Russell Kirk and Seymour M. Lipset. We were very conscientious in our effort to avoid the classroom intimidation of students and to allow all viewpoints to be expressed on emotional, intellectual, and even academic levels. Quite often our seminar sessions would be held off-campus in homes of professors and students to allow for a noninstitutional atmosphere and the informal exchange of ideas. These sessions normally met once a week with discussions lasting as long as four or five hours.

We encouraged our guest speakers to relate in terms of this give-and-take process. Question-and-answer periods usually lasted for a half-hour at the least and, in some cases, for over two hours. We were heavily criticized and, in fact, threatened for allowing certain speakers to be heard by our students. Dialogue necessitates freedom to express thoughts and feelings, to question without fear basic assumptions; and we believe the healthiest intellectual growth can come from the Socratic dialogue, which is so often stifled in univer-

sities today. Therefore, "freedom of speech" was not a relative concept, but a central theme of this experiment. We welcomed speakers
of all viewpoints and styles who related to the purpose of the course.

The approaches and backgrounds of contributions to this anthology are as diverse and spontaneous as is the student movement
itself. The phenomenon of university and revolution is a complex
one in which society and the university work outside and within
each other. The black revolt, the Vietnam war, and national politics
all affect the university. We cannot look at this particular mountain
from one angle, nor can we consider it without relating the mountain to its total environment. Each speaker gave us a deeper understanding of the university and revolution.

One of the primary problems involved in trying to understand the
student movement is lack of information regarding the American
philosophy of higher education and just what basic processes are
involved in running a university. The press has been severely criticized for its inability to report accurately on university turmoil.
Very often the public is presented with stories that relate only to
the violence of the student revolt without considering the issues or
root causes. Students are engaged in a fairly sophisticated "systems
analysis" of an institution which has been of little interest to the
average American. While students have become concerned with the
basic operations and purposes of the university, the public and the
press have displayed an astounding ignorance of these central issues.
Consequently, the press must literally create and present an entire
scenario before they can describe and explain why a particular revolt
took place. This is a job which requires too much newsprint of little
interest to readers. As with airplane news, only crashes are given
coverage, while successful flights, progressive changes, and the many
factors which cause crashes in the first place are neglected.*

People are faced with an ambiguous situation when viewing campus revolts. They therefore tend to judge the situation with a "rule
of thumb" (otherwise known as prejudice) that seeks to preserve
the *status quo,* ignoring the necessities for change and deeper un-

* In an address delivered at The American University, April 10, 1969,
Nicholas Von Hoffman of the *Washington Post* stressed many of the problems
involved in reporting university turmoil.

derstanding. We hope, through this collection, to broaden the criteria for judgment and lessen the confusion that exists. It is further hoped that our text will encourage other universities to develop courses of this nature.

G. R. W.

INTRODUCTION

Gary R. Weaver

In a January news interview with Howard K. Smith, former Vice President Humphrey commented that 1969 offered many prospects for peace because, he felt, the Vietnam conflict and civil disturbances had reached their peaks. Nevertheless, he cautioned that student uprisings had not subsided and would probably intensify. This prognosis has certainly proven true as campus after campus erupts in turmoil and Americans become increasingly alarmed with this rebellion. A March 1969 Gallup Poll found that campus disorders replaced the Vietnam war as the primary concern of Americans while Congress has begun debating how to control the university crisis without threatening the basic concept of academic freedom.

What has caused this turmoil? Why have students begun to challenge their own social, economic, and political systems? What are the goals and frustrations that provoke students to demand changes in such basic American institutions as the university, that create a "student movement"? [1] To answer any of these questions we

---

[1] The "student movement," as it is used in this introduction, refers to a large group of people, most of them under thirty, who are currently students or who identify themselves with the concept of a university community and see it as a legitimate focus for societal change. Thus the movement includes not only matriculated students but former students and persons who find the university milieu most congenial. They view educational institutions, traditional centers of critical thinking and dissent, as the most obvious arenas of change and as vanguards of socio-cultural values.

If the student movement can be said to be developing a class consciousness, it is a consciousness of responsibility for radically progressive change, traditionally the sphere of political "leftists." The "student left" is used to mean the vanguard of the movement. The entire movement, however, including its

must first decide upon the relationship between the university and society.

Robert Hutchins defines education as "the deliberate, organized attempt to help people to become intelligent":

> . . . It has no more practical aim. It does not have as its object the "production" of Christians, democrats, Communists, workers, citizens, Frenchmen, or businessmen. It is interested in the development of human beings through the development of their minds. Its aim is not manpower but manhood.[2]

This concept of education has generally been accepted since the beginnings of the first universities over 1,000 years ago, yet it has been continually challenged by the tendency of societal elites to use the university for more pragmatic purposes—to "produce" manpower through the nationalized industry of higher education. A root problem, then, is the constant threat to the ideal of an autonomous intellectual community posed by the demands of society.

In the United States, we have used universities as Xerox machines to reproduce the *status quo*—they have been cultural cookie-cutters taking as their pattern white, male, Anglo-Saxon, middle-class America. Previously as a university administrator and now as an instructor, I have often heard graduates referred to as "products" —"Myron Smith, now an IBM executive, is a *product* of the American University." The assumption is that the university parallels a factory which takes in homogeneous raw material and produces homogeneous products with the B.A. "Seal of Good Housekeeping."[3] We all know that human beings are *not* the same; they are not

---

vanguard, is intelligible only as an amalgamation of individuals who share a mood, a cultural revision without the structure and linear direction of a political ideology. One may discern Marxists, Neo-Trotskyites, pacifists, Democratic Socialists, Yippie "politicians of joy," Americans for Democratic Action, and a host of other traditional ideologues, but when one looks for a common political denominator it is nowhere to be found. The answer lies in the ambience of a generation born after the failure and death of ideology.

[2] Robert M. Hutchins, *The Learning Society* (New York: Frederick A. Praeger, Inc., 1968), p. viii.

[3] See Robert Theobald, *An Alternative Future for America* (Chicago: Swallow Press, Inc., 1968), p. 171.

homogeneous raw material, yet the university strives to remove these differences. In fact, I often wonder if the primary goal of the American university is to teach students to conform instead of allowing them to develop their individual preceptions, talents, indentities, and value systems, that is, to develop their manhood. For the black student this process is especially serious in that he must conform to the white mold into which he knows he can never fully fit. The problem of sacrificing manhood for manpower is even more serious because he has been deprived of his manhood for over 300 years. Blacks simply cannot accept this cookie-cutter pattern and they rebel against an educational system which teaches that the black man has had little, if any, impact on the culture in which he lives.[4]

One of the primary goals of students today is making Hutchins' definition of education a reality. They do not want to be processed and treated as products made to fulfill manpower demands. Instead, they wish to be considered as individuals who are being deliberately aided in becoming intelligent human beings. Students are shouting to their society to stop programming them as tools and to give them an opportunity to be independent, purposeful individuals. The search for individual identity and the anxiety of meaninglessness in a technological society has gone far beyond the internalized brooding of the 1950s and has erupted in radical expressions of rage on the university campus. The "rebel without a cause" now has a cause and rebels openly—almost pathologically—demanding his manhood and sense of individual identity.

The second most obvious characteristic of the student movement is a broad humanitarianism which very much resembles the Romantic movement in Europe. This seems to be a response to the extreme materialism and depersonalization that has resulted from the rapid changes of the technological era. Whereas the "lonely crowd" of the late 1950s sought to escape the responsibilities of utilizing technological power to make society both more humane and more human, the generation of the late 1960s is acting out the existential thinking of the Beat generation and has substituted

[4] Speech by Louis Lomax, delivered at The American University, April 11, 1969.

action for thought. There is certainly a diminution of the reverence for property as youth has begun to extol the worth of human relationships in a humane milieu. Poverty, war, discrimination, and violence are no longer vague abstractions as a student watches the evening news. For him body counts are once-living people, hunger statistics are starving children. While the generation of the 1950s was praising the development of business and technology, the present generation scorns these materialistic developments. In a sense, they are attempting to provoke the older generation to consider not only the fantastic technology and skill which could create a missile, but the destructive capabilities of that missile. In other words, the humane and human have become important considerations for these students.

Finally, students are demanding that the ideals of their society be implemented in the actions of that society. They are not willing to accept the hypocrisy of a society which preaches an idealism of the past while the actions of the present speak so loudly to the contrary that the ideology cannot be heard. Students have little reverence for the past or hope for the future—old moral victories and dreams of those to come are meaningless. They truly are the "now" generation who have learned the cynical truths of life very early—perhaps earlier than previous generations who were numbed by the greenhouse environment of sheltered homes, smaller communities, and limited mass communication. Because of the communications explosion, the truth can no longer be filtered out. Ironically, it is not so much a problem of two generations who disagree on values as a question of which generation will implement the values most honestly. Careful analysis of many of the leftist groups reveals elements of Thoreau and Jefferson, the Declaration of Independence, and the Bible.

Perhaps the severest criticism which can be made of the student left is that it is a reflection of American cultural values and often attempts to bring back the ideology of the eighteenth and nineteenth centuries. "Anarchism," self-determination, populism, and other such student-leftist watchwords are all part of the Western tradition. Today, however, we live in a mass democracy with sophisticated media and problems which are much more complex

than those of the eighteenth and nineteenth centuries. Town meet-
ings were perhaps the best mode of implementing American ideology at that time, but they are counterproductive in today's cyber-
netical society. The student left should be striving to find new
ways of implementing their values, ways relevant to the twentieth
century and to a post-technological society. Darwin, Marx, Freud,
and many other have confirmed that the public is prone to manipulation and often acts irrationally. With mass communications
and the Madison Avenue approach to selling public policy, students
should be creatively developing means to avoid the pitfalls of
utilizing an eighteenth-century methodology to realize their ideology. New structures, decision-making processes, and modes of
citizen participation must be devised. To return to historical clichés
and previous ideologies is regressive and will not help to make
the American society more democratic, more humane, or more
human.

Individualism, humanitarianism, and a sense that the political
and economic machinery of the United States is not effectively or
legitimately meeting the needs of its people—these are the core
components of the student left. But the picture is further complicated by the existence of another revolution which complements
the student left: the revolt of the "Underclass"—the poor, the
blacks, and other minority groups—which has shared many of the
student-left goals. The student left began with the civil rights
movement in the South. One could say that the civil rights movement helped the white students more than the black cause. It
politicized and brought life to the "Ungeneration" of the 1950s.
In fact, SDS (Students for Democratic Society) originated through
the efforts of such whites as Tom Hayden, Jack Newfield, and Carl
Oglesby, who came of age in radical politics during their years of
work in the Southern campaigns of the civil rights movement.

The "New Class" (the student body which now comprises a
larger proportion of our population than ever before) and the
"Underclass" are moving at the same time and in similar directions:
SNCC (Student Non-Violent Coordinating Committee) and SDS
were once closely allied on many issues, and today we still find
coalitions between the Peace and Freedom Party and the Black

Panthers. Although these coalitions are very often temporary and issue-oriented they are pragmatically initiated and leave open the possibility of integration on higher levels. Most importantly, however, they aim for the same ends. The Kerner Commission found that "Negro protest, for the most part, has been firmly rooted in the basic values of American society, seeking not their destruction but their fulfillment." [5] This same observation can be made of the student left.

Representative Shirley Chisholm (D–N.Y.) declared in April 1969, "Eventually a coalition of college students and black people will save American society." [6] This concept of the two movements working together is shared by some of those Black leaders commonly considered "separatist" in nature. Malcolm X observed:

> As racism leads America up the suicide path, I do believe that the whites of the younger generation, in the colleges and universities, will see the handwriting on the wall and many of them will turn to the spiritual path of truth—the only way left to America to ward off the disaster that racism inevitably must lead to. [7]

Eldridge Cleaver writes:

> There is in America a generation of white youth that is truly worthy of a black man's respect and this is a rare event in the foul annals of American History. . . . If a man like Malcolm X could change and repudiate racism, if I myself and other former Muslims can change, if young whites can change, then there is hope for America. It was certainly strange to find myself, while steeped in the doctrine that all whites were devils by nature, commanded by the heart to applaud and acknowledge respect for these young whites—despite the fact that they are descendants of the masters and I the descendant of the slave. The sins of the fathers are visited upon the heads

[5] *Report of the National Advisory Commission on Civil Disorders* ["The Kerner Report"] (New York: Bantam Books, 1968), p. 236.

[6] Shirley Chisholm, *The Washington Post*, April 17, 1969, p. B11.

[7] Malcolm X, *The Autobiography of Malcolm X* (New York: Grove Press, Inc., 1966), p. 341.

of the children—but only if the children continue in the evil
deeds of the fathers. . . .[8]

The examination of basic American concepts and values is shared
by the white youth and the black. Thus the first sit-in at a Greensboro lunch counter had whites join within 24 hours, and this sense
of shared values between the New Class and Underclass continues
today.

In addition to this expanding "coalition" between the New Class
and the Underclass, there is now a very strong reactionary response
in what might be termed the traditional middle class. It is possible
to interpret the Chicago Convention melée as a class war between
the New Class–Underclass coalition and the police, who represent
the lower middle class. The possibility of attending college is
often considered a luxury by police who had no opportunity for
higher education. Moreover, while the policemen's sons could not
evade the draft through educational deferments or other means
available to the wealthy, the student left openly defies the authority
of the police and abuses the luxury of attending college.

This reactionary response is also reflected in the legislative
sectors, especially on the state level, where numerous bills are
being written to control the campus revolts.[9] Most opinion polls
taken during periods of campus unrest have indicated that the
American public favors hard responses to student uprisings. And,
in response to civil disorders and student uprisings, President
Nixon's appeal to "law and order" became a short-term panacea
for many voters.

Many factors suggest, as of this writing, that the American
student revolt will not be suppressed, but will probably intensify
and become more violent. First, this is a "New Left" movement
with significant differences from the leftist movement of the 1930s,
which was indeed driven underground.[10] Neither leftist students

[8] Eldridge Cleaver, Soul on Ice (New York: McGraw-Hill Book Company,
A Ramparts Book, 1968), p. 83.

[9] See Chancellor Glenn S. Dumke's address in this volume, pp. 121–131. He
notes that there are strong repressive tendencies in the California and Wisconsin state legislatures.

[10] See Jack Newfield, A Prophetic Minority (New York: The New American
Library, Inc., Signet Books, 1967), pp. 109–30.

nor blacks strongly seek foreign answers to American problems, and the effect of these two movements is much more pervasive than that of the '30s.[11] There is a cultural revolution taking place which has brought into question all traditional art forms, language styles, and personal morals.[12] Although it may be possible to force the political end of the student left underground, the cultural components cannot be repressed. Thus, as we begin to question traditional sensory forms, it is but a matter of time before traditional political and social patterns also become open to question and change. As culturally formed sensory patterns become more flexible, it is probable that cognitive thought will also open up to new forms. The number of students who follow a form of ideology is small—one of the foremost characteristics of the student movement is its very lack of ideology, its spontaneity. To identify and repress those students who follow an "ideology" would have little effect on the total cultural movement taking place.[13]

Whether an outright "repression" is developing can be debated. One might argue that white students have entered this movement with a "creampuff mentality," naïvely thinking that they could pinch the establishment without getting slapped back for their actions. It is certainly true that many black students are suspicious of white sincerity. After all, blacks have felt a "suppression" much more clearly than white students—black students were shot in South Carolina and there were mass dismissals of black students at Oshkosh State in Wisconsin. Many blacks suspect that when the going gets rough white students will cry "repression" and return to their middle-class homes. Still, there is a crucial linkage between the two groups and any type of repressive action will prove inef-

[11] See Eldridge Cleaver's address in this volume, pp. 153–164.
[12] See Jack Newfield's address in this volume, pp. 43–54.
[13] See Edmund S. Glenn's address in this volume, pp. 99–118. Dr. Glenn views the student revolt as a cultural phenomenon which resembles the *Gemeinschaft–Gesellschaft* dichotomy. The students are asking for a more individualistic, community-oriented society while our technological age has necessitated an ordered society which defines a person as a citizen, disregarding his individual characteristics. Consequently, the dilemma of postindustrialization is that the individuality of man is sacrificed for the role that he plays as part of the societal team.

fective. The issues are too broad, the movement is more than simply a political ideology, and the great number of dissidents involved prevents their being extinguished as easily as previous leftist movements. In 1930 the college population was 1.5 million; today it is more than 7.5 million. Although the hard-core radical activists may constitute only 2 per cent of this total, this is a sizable number; to this should be added up to 40 per cent of the student population who support their causes. Combine this number with the black activists and it becomes apparent that the leftist movement today is large.

The second reason for believing that the student movement will probably intensify and become violent is that efforts to repress it will be met with more violent methodologies. Guerilla tactics are being seriously discussed by both blacks and whites. SDS has been actively pushing for confrontation on and off the college campus. In *The Washington Free Press* (April 1–15, 1969), diagrams for making Molotov cocktails and time bombs were featured. At San Francisco State a black student was seriously injured when a bomb exploded in his hands as he was placing it in a locker. Tactics similar to those of the Algerian revolution are also being employed by black militants. This is quite a step from the broadly nonviolent methods of the civil rights movements and the peace marches of the early 1960s. In the words of Eldridge Cleaver, who supports the alliance of blacks and white radical students:

> When the sane people don't do it, when all the good middle class people don't do it, then the madmen have to do it, and the madmen say that we're going to have freedom or we're going to have chaos; we're going to be part of the total destruction of America or we're going to be part of the liberation of America.[14]

Following the pattern of Eric Hoffer's analysis in *The True Believer*, the "men of action" have begun to replace the "men of words" in both the black and student movements. Carl Oglesby

[14] Eldridge Cleaver quoted in *The Washington Free Press*, April 27, 1969.

and Tom Hayden, intellectuals who began with the civil rights marches, are now being severely criticized by SDS for their mildness though they were founders of SDS. Eldridge Cleaver is now regarded as rather moderate by some members of the new black wave.[15] This cannot be attributed solely to actions of the movements themselves—the abdication of responsibility by decision-makers and the public to treat the issues involved seriously and imaginatively has left the way open for these stronger tactics. Stifling peaceful student protests has very often severely limited the options available for change. Thus the situation becomes ripe for militant radicals to take charge.

The fundamental question which we must deal with is not whether the students and blacks are becoming more violent, but rather how one brings about change in this society. The condemnation of violence has allowed the people and the politicians to avoid the problem of necessary change. Violence is only a symptom of deeper societal ills, and these symptoms cannot be treated without considering the root causes and their subtler psycho-sociological dynamics. It is possible to control the symptoms of migraine headache by considering only the physiological aspect of the illness; the root cause, however, often lies within the total psycho-sociological make-up of the individual.

One of the primary contributions of the left is that it has forced America to reconsider the question of violence and its use. The American ruling class—generally white and middle-class—has traditionally used violence to get what it wants. We did not behave nonviolently toward the British or the American Indians.[16] Even the destruction of one's own property is not new to America. When the Sons of Liberty dumped tea in Boston Harbor, they were destroying their own tea. We all know what the destruction of that tea meant, yet we cannot seem to understand what the destruction of the ghetto—and in some cases the university—means

---

[15] Norman Cousins, "Reflections on a Revolution," *Saturday Review* (May 17, 1969), p. 22.
[16] The question of violence and the concept of "law and order" were dealt with expertly by Louis Lomax in his address of April 11, 1969, at the American University.

today. This destructive outlet is most apparent for the black dis-
senter who does not find available the options for change that the
white youth has. As Dick Gregory has said in *The Shadow That
Scares Me:*

> America has refused to listen to the brilliant, natural voice of
> the ghetto and has preferred to pass judgment instead. The
> words of Jesus ring out to America, "You hypocrite, first take
> the log out of your eye, and then you will see clearly to take
> the speck out of your brother's eye." If America would observe
> the wounds she has inflicted in the ghetto, rather than judging
> the actions of the wounded, the social problem could be
> solved.[17]

The black man today is forcing America to examine whether it is
capable of preventive action or, as Erich Fromm states it, anticipatory change—those steps necessary to avoid the catastrophic
change which has engulfed other civilizations. So far, the evidence
is that we cannot anticipate change.

Albert Cleage, a black preacher from Detroit, perhaps best sums
up this concept of violence from the black man's point of view
when he says:

> America is set on a disaster course of conflict and violence.
> The black man cannot accept America as it is. The white man
> refuses to make the changes necessary for the black man to live
> in America with dignity and justice. These are two facts. We
> will not accept conditions as they are, and the white man will
> not accept change. There is no solution to that except open
> conflict and violence.[18]

Moreover, it is the *status quo* which is violent to the oppressed.
Students and blacks realize this and are aware that they have the
power to change a political, social, and economic system which
oppresses. The Kerner Commission reports:

[17] Dick Gregory, *The Shadow That Scares Me* (New York: Simon & Schuster,
1969), p. 89.
[18] Quoted in John Hersey, *The Algiers Motel Incident* (New York: Bantam
Books, Inc., 1968), p. 298.

A climate that tends toward the approval and encouragement of violence as a form of protest has been created by white terrorism directed against nonviolent protest, including instances of abuse and even murder of some civil rights workers in the South; by the open defiance of law and federal authority by state and local officials resisting desegregation.[19]

Status quo violence is much subtler—as a member of SDS has said, "How can a system be justified that manufactures eighteen different kinds of underarm deodorants and lets people in Harlem go hungry and get bitten by rats?"

De Tocqueville has commented that the evils which are endured with patience so long as they are incurable, seem intolerable as soon as hope can be entertained of escaping them. Today the evils of the ghetto, war, poverty, and discrimination have become intolerable while the mass media flaunt American affluence before the eyes of the deprived. The young and the blacks are aware of the possibility for curing these ills. They see clearly the moral duplicity of a society which has historically used violence to solve its problems yet condemns violence when "outsiders" use it.

This tendency to "judge the bleeding rather than treat the wound" [20] can be found over and over again on college campuses. Ewart Brown, student-body president and leader of the Howard University revolt in the spring of 1968, noted that students appealed to every legitimate channel available at the university to bring about change in their curriculum. They began with polite suggestions to administrators. These were ignored. Then memos were sent urging change. These were ignored. Finally students "demanded" that changes be made in the curriculum. The immediate response of the administration was a condemnation of the use of the word "demand." Even at this desperate hour, administrators chose to judge the wording and not respond to the issues involved. How many newspapers today really concern themselves with student issues rather than the sensationalism of potential

---

[19] *Report of the National Advisory Commission on Civil Disorders, op. cit.,* p. 205.
[20] Gregory, *op. cit.,* p. 90.

violence? During the American University revolt of Spring 1969 most newspapers ceased to cover the confrontation as soon as the possibility of violence was removed, yet most of the significant progress came quietly in reasoned discussions among administrators, students, and faculty.

The third reason for believing the student revolt will intensify is that students are beginning to challenge the political core of the university system—the faculty. Almost every administrator will admit that real power regarding curriculum change, personnel policies, admission requirements, and the like rests in the hands of the faculty. Today, students want to change these policies and procedures and become part of the decision-making process. No longer are demonstrations focusing on poor housing, curfews, or even administrators. They are beginning to challenge the present channels of decision-making and consequently are bringing into question such concepts as tenure and the distribution of monies. These are all political questions which have been within the realm of the faculty.

The tenure system came about to protect professors from administrators—to allow them to voice their opinions freely without the threat of dismissal. Today it has become an institutionalized way of preserving and protecting mediocrity. To allow student participation on decision-making bodies which "advise" administrators as to personnel policies and tenure is to remove this protective umbrella from tenured professors and, on the other hand, to save untenured professors from the threat of not receiving tenure from their colleagues.

Curriculum decisions are equally political in that knowledge is presently divided into compartments structured at least twenty years ago which are commonly referred to as "departments." Each department has a faculty and a budget which it protects by stressing the purity of its particular discipline. Present-day awareness of the complexities of the world and increased access to information lead students to question the uniqueness of this artificial categorization of knowledge. They know that one cannot understand psychological problems without understanding the sociological structuring of society. They know that economics influences political decisions.

And they want to apply knowledge to the world and its problems. Thus curricula must become more issue-oriented and interdisciplinary. To achieve this, however, is to threaten professors and present budgetary structuring. Thus resistance will be extremely high.

One of the foremost clichés regarding the desire of students to become involved in the university decision-making process is the rhetorical question, "Should the patients run the hospital?" For one thing, only the small minority of student ideologues would ask to have control over or "run" a university. One could respond with an analogous and equally simplistic question, "Can penal reform be initiated by the jailers?" The input of student opinion and judgment is crucial to change in the university and it is doubtful that significant change will be brought about solely through faculty initiative. The preservation of the *status quo* is of paramount concern to the faculty. As in a jail, students are the prisoners, transitory guests whose thought is to be disciplined by the jailers. If they perform well and conform to the expectations of the jailers, they will be released after four years. The concern of the jailers is not necessarily to reform the prisoners, but instead to perpetuate their own convenience and autonomy. This analogy is even more appropriate today, when students are literally forced to attend college to survive in the technological world and, in many cases, to avoid participating in a war they deem unjust and immoral.

The student left and the black movement have brought into question the operation of many of our basic institutions, including both the university and the church. Both of these institutions should ideally promote movement toward the implementation of our ideals and develop forums for criticizing our society if we fail to follow our cultural mythology. There is no doubt that the tendency of both has been to reflect the society within which they exist rather than leading it to change with a radically changing environment. Both institutions should be beacons and not mirrors of their society. Students and blacks are reminding us of this very basic role of American institutions.

Furthermore, these movements are forcing us to re-examine basic American concepts such as the role of violence, equality, and the recently popularized cliché, "law and order." I suggest that these concepts have been discussed in mass media as a reaction to the changes which youth and blacks are demanding. Nixon and other politicians have been waving the flag of the *status quo*.

The concept of "law and order" is perhaps the major bastion of the *status quo* which students and blacks have brought into question. The white establishment that spawned this cliché is being rejected by its own children and by blacks. The question these dissidents are forcing the American people to ask is "Whose law, what order?" [21] Why is it that the chants of "law and order" have arisen today? All of those years when black bodies were floating down the Mississippi and hanging from swamp trees, no one asked for "law and order." Let us consider the following quote, which comes from one of the foremost creators and supporters of law and order:

> The streets of our country are in turmoil. The universities are filled with students rebelling and rioting. Communists are seeking to destroy our country. Russia is threatening us with her might. And the republic is in danger. Yes, danger from within and without. We need law and order. Yes, without law and order our nation cannot survive. . . . Elect us and we shall restore law and order.

Although this rings with the familiar tone of the Nixon and Wallace presidential campaigns, it comes from none other than Adolf Hitler in Hamburg, Germany in the year 1932! Certainly the law and order of the South has oppressed the black man as much as the pre-World War II law and order of Germany did the Jew. Whose law and what order was Hitler speaking about?

In 1967 Mayor Cavanaugh of Detroit observed, "When a substantial number of people in a community come to feel that law and order is their enemy and their oppressor, that community is in danger. Such groups exist in most of our communities today." [22] The point these blacks and students are making is that without

---

[21] Lomax, *op. cit.*
[22] Hersey, *op. cit.*, p. 276.

justice there can be no law or order. If we ask, "Whose law, what order?" we are faced with considering the concept of justice and the statement of Christ, "Man was not made for the law; the law was made for man." I suggest that the "law and order" cliché has recently become popularized because the changes which blacks and students are asking our society to make require us to evaluate the justice of our actions internally and externally. In the spirit of Thoreau and Emerson they are challenging America to re-examine the relationship between law and man and to change those institutions which do not protect all citizens or allow them to exercise their rights.

Indeed we are living in an age of rebellion. By definition, man is a rebel—he assaults the prison he is born into. As Robert Lindner so well points out: Man adapts alloplastically to his environment—most animals make autoplastic adaptation. Thus, rebellion actually defines man.[24] Today, our institutional structure is being assaulted on political, moral, and philosophic levels. Yet, to understand and cope with the technological environment we must have a positive revolt aimed at discovering new answers to the questions of the quantity and quality of life. Our technological growth has outpaced our socio-psychological ability to cope with it because training, not education, has become increasingly important in our postindustrial society. The task of the university is not to bury youth in an information overload, but to combine this transmission of information with interpretation, with methods of handling that information. Education must foster creativity, and redefine the mythology of our culture to make it real and relevant to individual needs while benefiting mankind in general.

Unfortunately, those who do not welcome this rebellion are supplying few alternatives and creative answers, while those who support the rebellion often adopt simplistic panaceas and tactics

[24] Robert Lindner, *Must You Conform?* (New York: Grove Press, Inc., 1961), p. 138. Most animals survive by adjusting or changing themselves with the demands of the environment while man attempts to conquer his environmental limitations. Thus, instead of meeting environmental problems and frustrations by changing oneself (autoplastic adaptation), man has learned to rebel against his environment and, in fact, alter it (alloplastic adaptation).

dictated by impatience. As we have seen, the student left is characterized by spontaneity and lack of ideology. Yet, today we find some elements of the student left and black movement speaking in terms of political ideology instead of the previous political analysis. A closed-mindedness is rapidly polarizing both the right and left.

It is the responsibility of our institutions to allow for dialogue and creative responses to societal problems. The rebellion today demands that America either "practice what it preaches, or preach what it practices," as Malcolm X would put it. The generation of the 1950s internalized its frustrations with modern society, leading it to societal suicide—escapism in the forms of the beat generations and the existentialists. The generation of the 1960s is action-oriented—it acts out many of these same frustrations which have, however, become magnified in a period of domestic and international crisis. The university is part of the total revolution taking place in America today and is beginning to accept its role of providing critical analysis of the society. Perhaps it will be able to promote and direct anticipatory change if it can begin to educate instead of to train, to develop manhood instead of manpower, and to develop intellectuals instead of technicians.

The student revolt is taking place in our "best" universities and is often led by our "best" students. These are not irresponsible hippies, but bright, sensitive young people who want to share the responsibilities they feel their society and its institutions have abdicated. Certainly this is healthier and more mature than the panty-raids, goldfish-swallowing, and telephone-booth stuffing that took place in the 1950s while war was brewing, McCarthy was purging, discrimination and poverty were increasing, and individualism was being suppressed. The university may truly be relating to society by promoting change in a mass democracy and making the norms of our culture relevant to its practices. Students are making the university and revolution one and the same by concerning themselves with broad human issues and actually taking on the responsibility of criticizing society. If we can listen to these voices and accept their right to be heard, we may very well avoid the catastrophic change which the modern world is forcing upon us.

AMERICAN STUDENT ACTIVISM

Seymour M. Lipset[1]

I

Any effort to interpret the changing political behavior of American students in recent years is subject to the difficulty that it is dealing with a local aspect of a worldwide phenomenon. Although the events which precipitated student activism vary from country to country, and the targets of student attack differ, there are more common themes than differences in the tactics and ideologies of the movements. Unlike the youth and student movements of the 1930s, which were linked to adult political parties, the dominant ones of the present constitute a genuine youth rebellion, one which is almost as much levied against the major parties of the left, and the Soviet Union, as it is against the moderates and conservatives. The lack of involvement in adult politics has given free rein to the propensity of youth to adhere to absolute principles, to engage in expressive rather than instrumental politics. Little concerned with the immediate consequences of their actions, the New Left student movements appear ready to attack all existing structures, including the university, and to use tactics which alienate the majority, in order to make manifest their contempt, their total rejection of the intolerable world created by their elders. This rejection of respon-

[1] This article appeared as an introductory essay in *Student Politics and Higher Education of the United States: A Selected Bibliography* by Philip G. Altbach, published by United Ministries in Higher Education, St. Louis, Missouri and Center for International Affairs, Harvard University, Cambridge, Massachusetts, 1968. Portions have also appeared in the Fall, 1968 issue of *The Public Interest*—Eds.

sibility characterizes student groups in Japan, France, Germany, the United States, and many other countries.

To understand the reasons why the relatively passive postwar generation has been replaced by one which contains an activist minority of the "enraged," it is important to note the extent to which some of the conditions which dampened ideological controversy during the '40s and '50s have changed. Essentially, the politics of the two earlier decades were dominated first by World War II and then by the Cold War. Given a high degree of support among liberal intellectuals concerning these events, many who were deeply critical of various domestic institutions and practices found themselves defending the fundamental character of their societies as moral and decent against the totalitarian critics. For a brief period, historically speaking, Western democratic intellectuals found themselves engaging in actions which belied their role as critics. This period was broken by changes within communist society, as well as increasing awareness of the social conditions existing in the third underdeveloped world. The breakdown of monolithic communism, the rise of liberal opposition tendencies in various Eastern countries, the intensity of the Sino–Soviet split, all served to undermine the conviction that all men of good will and all noncommunist nations must unite to fight totalitarian expansionism. In a real sense, the Cold War came to an end.

This change had considerable impact on those members of the older generation who had remained liberal critics, but had kept quiet either because they agreed with the assumptions justifying unity against the communist threat, or because they feared social or political sanctions from the supporters of anticommunism. Many of them had been active when younger in various radical movements, and though publicly quiescent had continued their criticisms within private circles. As a group, they were concentrated among college-educated professionals and intellectuals, including particularly university faculties. Jews as a group had been relatively heavily involved in radical activities in the 1930s and '40s, a phenomenon which stemmed from continuity with the political values brought over from the ghettoes of eastern Europe, from experience with domestic anti-Semitism which was particularly strong in the United States until the end of World War II, and from an identification of Nazism with conservatism and militant anti-communism. As ideological anticommunism lost strength, the former radicals and left liberals returned in some measure to their earlier beliefs. More significant, however, was the emergence among younger intellectuals and students of widespread social criticism, sentiments which were often encouraged by their "liberated" elders. The new generations of liberals who knew not Hitler and Stalin, the Czech coup, and the Hungarian revolution from firsthand experience, found little reason to restrain applying their moral beliefs to politics.

II

This change in ideological climate, as well as the rather rapid escalation of protest from words to action, was facilitated by the struggle for Negro rights which emerged in the years following the Supreme Court's school desegregation decision of 1954. This was the perfect issue around which to create a new activist movement, since it engaged the principal aspect of American society, in which the system engaged in actions which were at sharp variance with its manifest creed of equality and democracy. Most Americans, and the university system *in toto*, recognized that Negro inequality is evil, and in principle approved all actions designed to reduce or eliminate it. Hence race was the easiest issue around which the new political criticism could mobilize. To organize to fight segregation, particularly in the South, was not a radical act. Yet the struggle contributed greatly to radicalizing sections of the young. In this particular situation, the conservative or traditionalist forces introduced the tactics of civil disobedience, and even of violence, i.e., the Southern segregationists refused to accept the law as laid down by the Supreme Court and Congress, and taught the advocates of civil rights, both the black community and white students, that the regular peaceful methods of democracy would not work. The confrontationist tactics of civil disobedience, which first emerged in the South, were then diffused by the American student movement to other parts of the country and the world, and to other issues both inside and outside of the university.

The aggressive tactics of the civil rights movement were successful as judged by the criteria of actions taken by different agencies of government to outlaw discrimination and to foster economic and educational improvements. Whatever the profound limitations of these, the fact remains that more has been attempted by government to improve the situation of the Negro in recent years than in all the preceding years since Reconstruction. Many of these actions, particularly by the Administration, Congress, and local agencies, can be credited as responses to political militancy or the fear of ghetto riots. But though these efforts attest to the value of political action, they have not resulted in any major visible change in the position of the bulk of Negroes. They remain poor, segregated, and uneducated, securing the leavings of the labor market. To each group of civil-rights-concerned youth who have come to political consciousness during this period, the gap between what ought to be and what actually exists appears to have increased rather than decreased. They take for granted the existing structure, including the changes which had been made, and react with outrage against the continued sources of Negro deprivation. Older liberals, on the other hand, have often reacted with pleasure at the considerable progress that has been made within the past few years. Thus an inevitable age-related split has occurred. This division between the generations has been particularly acute within the Negro community. To younger Negroes, the gains made since the 1950s appear empty in the face of the existing pattern of Negro social and economic inferiority. And on the major campuses of the nation, the growing minority of Negro students have found themselves in a totally white-dominated world, facing few, if any, black faculty, and a white student body whose liberal and radical wing turned increasingly after 1964 from involvement in civil rights protest to activity directed against the Vietnam war. The concern with black power, with Negro control over their own communities, and particularly civil rights organizations has won growing support among black college students. Most recently, these students have played a major role in confronting university administrations with demands for more Negro students and faculty and for changes in the curriculum. Black students have been among the major forces initiating sit-ins during the 1967–68 school year at schools as diverse and separated as San Francisco State College, Columbia University, Boston University, Northwestern University, and many predominantly Negro institutions as well.

The issue of the acceptable pace of reform also has been affected by events abroad, particularly in Cuba and Vietnam. The triumph of the Castro movement, an event dominated by young men, produced an example of a revolution seemingly uncontaminated by Stalinism. Cuban events helped to generate the sense that revolution was both possible and desirable as a way to eliminate social evils. Again generational differences divided the liberal-left communities. The older ones had learned from experience that revolutions could lead to totalitarianism, to new intense forms of exploitation and to cynical betrayals of the popular will. To many youth, raising such matters seemed only to justify inaction against the intolerable aspects of the *status quo*.

The spread of opposition to the Vietnam war has, of course, become the dominant political issue affecting student activism. To the older generation, including initially most liberals, Vietnam was but the most recent episode in a two-decade-long struggle against communist imperialist expansion. To the new generations of the children of liberals and former radicals, Vietnam became defined in terms which placed American actions at odds with certain basic American beliefs, those of anti-imperialism, of the right of self-determination of politically weak peoples. Given the existence of a polycentric divided communism, it simply did not make sense to perceive Vietnamese communism as an extension of Russian or Chinese power. The very failure of the powerful United States quickly to defeat its small poor Vietnamese opposition has been evidence of the oppressive character of the war, of its being a war in which a foreign power seeks to impose its will by force over another people. The very values which led Americans to be suspicious of, and opposed to, the British, French, and Dutch empires,

and which were called into play to justify World Wars I and II and
the Korean War, have now been turned against the United States.

III

A general analysis of the changing political climate as it has
encouraged student dissatisfaction, of course, does not explain
why students qua students have played such an important role in
stimulating protest. Here it must be noted that students have
almost invariably been more responsive to political trends, to
changes in mood, to opportunities for social change than any other
group in the population, except possibly intellectuals. As a result
students have played a major role in stimulating unrest and foster-
ing change in many countries. The special role of students has been
particularly noted in the revolutions of 1848; in the Russian revolutionary movement which was largely a student one until 1905; in
the various Chinese movements during the first quarter of the
twentieth century; in the different fascist movements in Italy, Germany, and Spain, before they took power; in a host of colonial
and underdeveloped states; and in various communist countries
since 1956.

Historically then, one would expect a sharp increase in student
activism whenever events call accepted political and social values
into question, in times particularly where policy failures seem to
question the adequacy of social, economic, and political arrangements and institutions. Although it may be argued that student
activism is the result rather than the cause of social discontent, it
is important to recognize that once activated, student groups have
played a major role in mobilizing public opinion behind the causes
and ideologies fostered by them. Social unrest causes student unrest, but once they start expressing their disquiet, students and
intellectuals have been in many ways the vanguard of political
change.

Awareness of the important role of students has led to efforts to
detail those aspects of the situation of students generally, as well
as in specific times and places, which press them to act politically.

The factors to which attention has been called in the growing literature on the subject may be differentiated between those which motivate students to action and those which facilitate their participation.

Among the first are the frustrating elements in the student role. Students are, by occupation, marginal men. They are in transition between having been dependent on their families for income, status, and various forms of security and protection, and taking up their own roles in jobs and families. Studenthood is inherently a tension-creating period. The rapid growth in the number of students, 7 million today as compared with 1.5 million at the end of the 1930s, means both that the composition of the college population, as a group, has come from increasingly less privileged families, and that the value of a college degree for status placement has declined.

The university has become more meritocratic; it is how well you do, rather than who you are that counts. Hence, young people in a society in which education increasingly determines how well they start in the struggle for place find themselves facing a highly competitive situation. The pressures to conform to the requirements of the education establishment begin for many middle-class and aspiring working-class youth in elementary school and intensify in high school. Hard work and ability at each level only serve to qualify the individual to enter an even more difficult competition at the next rung in the educational ladder. While some succeed, many must show up as mediocre or must rank low.

There is a variety of evidence which suggests that these tensions affect the emotional stability of many teenagers and college youth, even the most able among them. Such tensions may find varying outlets, of which a rejection of the competitive social system which forces them into a rat race for grades is one. Although such tensions have always been present in the student role, it should be noted that they have intensified considerably in the last decade and a half. The very expansion of the numbers going to universities throughout the world has made the situation worse, more competitive, than before.

The idealism of youth, to which reference is frequently made, is another stimulating factor which is an outgrowth of social expectations. Societies teach youth to adhere to the basic values of the system in absolute terms: equality, honesty, democracy, socialism, and the like. There is a maxim which exists in various forms in many countries: "He who is not a radical at twenty does not have a heart; he who still is one at forty does not have a head." This statement is usually interpreted as a conservative one, assuming radicalism is an unintelligent response to politics. But the first part of the maxim may be even more important than the second, for it denotes a social expectation that young people should be radicals, that the older generation believes that youthful radicalism is praise-worthy behavior. It is the young conservative, the young "fogie," not the young radical who is out of step with social expectations. The emphasis on youthful reformism is even greater in the United States than in many other countries, for American culture places a premium on being youthful and on the opinions of youth. It tends in general to glorify youth and to deprecate age.

Many American adults are reluctant, even when they consciously disagree, sharply to call students or youth to task. Rather they may encourage youth and students to take independent new positions, rather than emphasize the worth of experience. This ties in with the part of the American self-image which assumes that the United States is a progressive country, one which accepts reform and change. And the truism that the youth will inherit the future is linked with the sense that the youth are the bearers of the progres-sive ideas which will dominate the future, that youth will contribute to the enduring struggle to make the American creed of equality more meaningful.

The real world, of course, necessarily deviates considerably from the ideal, and part of the process of maturing is to learn to operate in a world of conflicting values, roles, interests, and demands. Such compromises as this requires are viewed by youth as violations of basic morality. Students hang on to such beliefs longer than others. They tend, as Max Weber suggested, to develop an ethic of "absolute ends" rather than of "responsibility." They tend to be committed to ideals rather than institutions. Hence, those events which point up the gap between ideals and reality stimulate them to action.

Modern societies, moreover, are characterized by a prolongation of adolescence, usually devoted to educational development. Although physiologically mature, and often above the age legally defined as adult, students are expected to refrain from full involvement in the adult world. The very nature of university education is seen as calling for a withdrawal by the institution from the mainstream of society into an ivory tower, free from the constraints of politics and religion. Although living in a society which stresses that adults should establish their own status based on their individual abilities and achievements, students are expected to maintain a status in limbo, or to remain dependent on their family status. Such a situation can be highly frustrating, especially in a culture like the American, which places so much stress on individual achievement. Thus the student, in addition to the opportunity to acquire an education, also requires the chance both to experiment with adult roles and to exhibit his ability to achieve a position on his own.

Dependency is, of course, built into the very essence of the university system. Students are dependent as to the chances of their future placement on their standing with the faculty. The faculty has the power of certification through its control over grades. This gives them the right to influence what students read and how they spend much of their time. The American university, in particular, with its stress on frequent examinations and faculty judgments, emphasizes this dependent relationship even more than does that of most other countries. The American system of higher education has remained closer to that of the high school. Hence, the student who leaves home to attend university finds that he remains in a highly controlled situation, while many aspects of the society urge him to become independent.

The constraints imposed on students living in university dormitories have proved to be particularly onerous. By acting *in loco parentis*, universities in America took on the role of constraining agent over the social life of individuals who increasingly have claimed the right to be autonomous. And in a world in which eighteen-year-olds are eligible for the draft, the effort of the university to maintain these controls has been inevitably doomed to failure. With the decline in average age at which Americans reach sexual maturity from a physical point of view, and the accompanying changes in the accepted norms concerning sexual relations, the university has placed itself in the impossible position of seeking to enforce a status of social dependency which even middle-class parents have found difficult to maintain.

It may be argued that student life in general, and student activism in particular, are among other things an expression of youth culture. The student stratum, as such, tends to create a whole array of age-group symbols, which sets it apart from others in society, and from adults in particular. These include unique patterns of personal appearance, peculiar modes of communication, and special styles of life (relatively low standard of living, but major expenditures on music or travel, or use of drugs as compared with adults' consumption of liquor). Political extremism, the formation of student political groups which are unaffiliated with or at odds with adult political parties, would seem to be another example of such behavior.

IV

Involvement in university life makes politics a particularly critical source of self-expression. Students are given ample opportunity to discuss and study political matters. The university itself, in spite of its emphasis on academic freedom and on being nonpartisan, is increasingly involved in politics, as professors fulfill ever-growing roles as party activists, intellectual commentators on political events, advisors, consultants, and as researchers on policy-relevant matters. Many students are thus in centers of great political significance, but have little or no share in the political status of the university. Much of faculty political involvement, although generally on the left of the spectrum in the United States, occurs within the establishment. Hence, if it is to express a sense of separate identity, student politics as part of the student culture must be outside of and in opposition to that of most of the adults.

Although the student protest is directed against much of the adult world, including the faculty, it is important to note that changes in the backgrounds and opinions of increasing numbers of college faculty have undoubtedly had considerable impact on their students. Before the 1930s the American professoriate was not known especially for having strong political views or for engaging in political action. This changed somewhat during the Depression with the identification of the New Deal with reliance on academic expertise. Since World War II particularly, various segments of the population with strong liberal views, which hitherto played very small roles in university life, finally moved in a massive way onto the campus.

The university has become a major occupational outlet for many of the brightest people who seek to be innovative and free of the ideological restrictions and materialistic commitments which they believe inherent in the corporate and professional worlds. Once liberals entered the university, their influence tended to be self-accelerating. The militant "New Deal liberals" and exponents of "modernist" culture have been able to change the entire temper of the university. Evidence drawn from a variety of surveys of student attitudes indicates that colleges have a liberalizing effect on young people, particularly in areas linked to universalistic principles, racial equality, internationalism, peace, class relationships, as well as in more personal beliefs such as religion and sexual behavior. Samuel Stouffer pointed out over ten years ago that the conservatives who attack the universities for "corrupting" young people are right from their political and moral standpoints.

But if faculty help to create a climate of opinion which presses students to the left, ironically, at least some of the sources of student malaise stems from the fact that changes in the role of the faculty have contributed to making the situation of being a student less attractive than it once was. With increasing size and greater pressures on faculty to do research, publish, and take part in extramural activities, inherently one should expect to find poorer instruction, more faculty aloofness, and administrative indifference to students. The research-oriented faculty increasingly give a larger proportion of their limited teaching time to graduate students. University administration involves fund-raising, lobbying public officials, handling of research contracts, and concern for recruiting and retaining prestigious faculty. There can be little doubt that undergraduate students, as such, are of much less concern to the faculty and administration than in earlier periods of American education.

The very increase in the importance of the university as a center of influence and power, and as the major accrediting institution of the society, has reduced the informal influence of students within the university. The higher estates of the university, administrators, and faculty, however, have sought to maintain their traditional authority and prerogatives, while reducing their own "responsibility" for the quality of the personal and intellectual lives of their students. This development is not simply or even principally a function of the growth of the university; it reflects even more the increased "professionalization" of the faculty, the extent to which "teaching" as such has declined as the main identification of the role of being a professor.

The changes in the role of the faculty, their increased involvement in a national prestige system (based on evaluations of their scholarly achievements or extramural activities), the sharp increase in their income (derivative in large part from the fact that many schools are in competition for those who have or promise to attain general reputations), and the concomitant decline in faculty teaching obligations have not necessarily made for a "happier" professoriate. Faculty, like students, are in an increasingly competitive situation, one in which men see themselves being judged as to their position in national and local pecking orders. While some succeed in becoming nationally recognized figures, most faculty necessarily turn out to be failures in the struggle for scholarly status. With the depreciation of the teaching function as a local source of economic reward and status, many who have lost out in the competition within their own generation, or who, if successful, fear or actually see younger men coming up and securing the status they once had, become deeply dissatisfied and anxious. The universities and colleges, which are increasingly competitive with each other in efforts at stockpiling distinguished scholars, encourage such feelings among both their older and younger faculty by invidiously rewarding, often in a very public fashion, those men who are most valuable in this race for institutional prestige. Such sentiments reinforce faculty propensities to oppose the administrations of their schools, as well as the dominant values and institutions of the larger society. Hence, many professors find solace in student militancy directed against the forces they hold responsible for their felt sense of status inferiority or insecurity. The same faculty members who demand and secure lower teaching loads (ironically especially after student revolts which further reduce the "bargaining strength" of the university) often tell their students that they are neglected and misused by the administration and trustees.

V

It may be argued that American students, as students, are subject to greater strains and less rewards than those of previous generations, with the exception of the Depression generation. Although the demand for "student power," for increased influence by students over the decision-making process in the university, tends on the whole to be raised by the left-wing activist groups, the receptivity which this demand secures in wider circles of students may reflect the increased sense of grievance that the university demands more yet gives less in the form of personal relations (informal influence) among students, faculty, and administration. Thus, as in the case of workers and employees in bureaucratized industry, a sort of student syndicalism would seem to be emerging which seeks to regain symbolically for students as a group the influence which they have lost individually as a result of changes in the organization of universities.

Conversely, the often unconceptualized sense of grievance with their situation, a sense which in many cases is now consciously directed against the university, also may make many students, particularly those with a politically critical background, more receptive to political action directed against trends in the larger society. The two sources of activism thus reinforce one another; the more directly political uses campus discontent to create a set of issues around which to build a movement, while campus discontent may express itself in wider political issues. These are general aspects of student motivation to activism. There are many aspects in the situation of the group which facilitate mass activity, which make it easier to recruit them for such action.

Young people are more available for new political movements than adults. As new citizens, as people entering the political arena, they are less committed to existing ideologies, they have few or no explicit political commitments, they have no previous personal positions to defend, they are less identified with people and institutions which are responsible for the *status quo*. Inherently, they know less recent history than adults. For this current generation, as noted earlier, the key formative events in foreign policy terms have been the Vietnam war, and domestically, in the United States, heightened awareness of the oppressed position of the American Negroes.

Students are also more available because of the lesser commitments they have to their "occupational" role as compared to adults. Max Weber many years ago pointed out that political activity is to a considerable extent a function of the extent to which job requirements are dispensable or not. In his terms, those who could take time off from work without suffering economic consequences are much more likely to be active than those who have to punch a timeclock. Students (and professors) have perhaps the most dispensable job requirements of all. Students may drop out of school, may put off their studies for short or long periods, without paying a great price. They may often delay taking examinations. The numbers who dropped their books to take part in Senator Eugene McCarthy's campaign for nomination are a recent illustration of this.

Linked with this is the factor of "responsibility." As compared with other groups, students simply have fewer responsibilities in the form of commitments to families and jobs. Thus the existence of punitive sanctions against extremist activism is less likely to affect students than those with greater responsibilities to others, or to a career ladder. Moreover, as noted earlier, students remain adolescents or juveniles sociologically, and they are often implicitly treated as such legally, particularly when they violate the law. In many societies, a number of the students involved in politically or otherwise-motivated infractions are literally the children of the elite, a fact which serves to reduce the will to punish them. In addition, universities are generally run by liberal individuals who are not inclined to invoke severe sanctions against students. Students are under less pressure to conform than other groups.

Another factor which facilitates student political involvement is the physical situation of the university, which makes it relatively easy to mobilize students who are disposed to act politically. The campus is the ideal place in which to find large numbers of people in a common situation. Many universities have over 30,000 students concentrated in a small area. New ideas which arise as a response to a given issue may move readily among the students, and find their maximum base of support. Only a small percentage of the massive bodies are necessary to make a large demonstration. Thus in 1965–67, although opinion polls indicated that the great majority of American students supported the Vietnam war, that antiwar sentiment within the group was no greater than in the population as a whole, the campus opposition was able to have a great impact because it could be mobilized. The antiwar student minority could and did man impressive antiwar demonstrations. During 1967–68, as the country as a whole turned increasingly critical of the war, campus opinion, both student and faculty, has moved to a majority antiwar position. This has placed the student antiwar activist groups in a very strong position, comparable to the one held earlier by the civil rights organizations; their goals, if not always their means, are approved by the community within which they operate.

It remains true, as Herbert Marcuse pointed out recently, that the majority of the students in all countries are politically quiescent and moderate in their views. According to national surveys of student opinion taken by the Harris Poll in 1965 and the Gallup Poll in 1968, approximately one-fifth of American students have participated in civil rights or political activities (17 per cent in 1964–65, the year of the Berkeley revolt, and 20 per cent in 1967–68, the year of the McCarthy and Kennedy campaigns). Despite the increasing opposition to the Vietnam war among students, only 7 per cent of a 1968 Gallup survey of American students indicated that they would refuse to serve if drafted. The radical activist groups generally have tiny memberships. The American New Left Students for a Democratic Society (SDS) claims a total membership of about 30,000 (of whom 6,000 pay national dues) out of a national student body of 7 million. A Harris Poll of American students taken in the spring of 1968 estimates that there are about 100,000 radical activists, or somewhere between 1 and 2 per cent of the college population.

The opinion surveys of American students indicate that the large majority are not sympathetic with radical doctrines and tactics. Yet the activist elements, both liberals and leftists, dominated the political tone of many campuses and have played a major role in influencing American politics in the 1960s. Given the fact that the activists are a relatively small minority, the question must be raised as to who they are and what the factors are which contribute to activist strength.

VI

The major conclusion to be drawn from a large number of studies in the U.S.A. and other countries is that leftist students are largely the children of leftist or liberal parents. The activists, particularly, are more radical or activist than their parents, but both parents and children are located on the same side of the spectrum. Conversely, studies of those active in conservative student groups, like the Goldwaterite Young Americans for Freedom (YAF), indicate that they are largely from rightist backgrounds. Students are more idealistic and committed than their parents, but generally in the same direction.

In line with these findings, the available data indicate that the student left is disproportionately Jewish. Adult Jews are overwhelmingly liberal or radical. Studies of activists at the Universities of Chicago, Wisconsin, Columbia, and California, all report that Jewish participation in leftist activism has far outweighed their proportion in the student body.

Intellectuals, academics, writers, musicians and so forth tend as a group to be disproportionately on the left. They are either liberal Democrats, or supporters of left-wing minor parties. And studies of student populations suggest that students who are intellectually oriented, who identify as "intellectuals," or who aspire to intellectual pursuits after graduation, are also much more prone to be on the left and favorable to activism than those inclined to business and professional occupations.

Among faculty and students, there are clearcut correlations between disciplines and political orientations. On the whole those involved in the humanities and social sciences, or in the more pure theoretical fields of science, are more likely to be on the left than those in the more practical, applied, or experimental fields. Such variations, however, would appear to be more a product of selective entrance into different disciplines than of the effects of the content of the fields on those pursuing them as students or practitioners. Thus studies of entering freshmen report the same relationships between intended college major and political attitudes as are found among seniors, graduate students, and faculty. Morris Rosenberg, who conducted a panel study (repeat interviews with the same people two years apart) of students reported that political orientation proved to be a major determinant of shifts in undergraduate major. A large proportion of the minority of conservatives who chose liberal (in political terms) majors as freshmen changed to subjects studied by conservatives, while many liberals who had selected conservative majors tended to shift to fields which were presumably more congenial with their political outlook.

The relationships between academic fields and political sympathies are also linked to the finding that the leftist activists within American universities tend to come from relatively well-to-do backgrounds as compared to the student population generally. A comparison by Braungart and Westby of the delegates to conventions of SDS and YAF also indicated that the left-wingers come from somewhat more affluent backgrounds than the rightists. The majority of the latter are the children of conservative businessmen and professionals, but they include a significant proportion—one-fifth—from working-class origins, a group almost unrepresented among the SDS delegates. In general, studies of the social backgrounds of students in different disciplines suggest that those who major in the liberal arts subjects and have an intellectual or scholarly bent have well-educated parents; while first-generation college students of working-

class origins tend to be vocationally oriented in a narrow sense—
they are more likely to be found among those preparing to become
engineers, businessmen, and the like. First-generation college students come disproportionately from that segment of the less privileged which is strongly oriented toward upward mobility and the
values of the privileged. Their strong concentration on professional
objectives, plus the need of many of them to hold a job during the
school term, also results in these students being less available for
political activities than those from more privileged families. These
findings not only hold up within schools, but may also help to explain the fact that colleges attended by large numbers of less well-
to-do students, Negroes apart, are less likely to be strongholds of
left-wing groups than those which educate the scions of the upper-
middle class.

The political character of certain schools also may be linked to
other sources of selective recruitment and the resultant political
orientation of their students. Those with a large number of well-to-do
Jewish students—or currently, with the rise of Negro militancy, of
black students—tend to be centers of leftist students oriented toward
becoming intellectuals. Thus we may account for the pattern of student protest at schools like Reed, Swarthmore, Antioch and others.
The best state universities, as judged in terms of faculty scholarly
prominence—e.g., California, Michigan, and Wisconsin—are also
schools which have become the most important centers of confrontationist politics. These schools attract a disproportionate number of
intellectually oriented students, including many Jews.

The political traditions and images of certain universities also may
play an important role in determining the orientation of their students and faculty. In the United States, Madison—seat of the University of Wisconsin—and Berkeley have maintained records as
centers of radicalism. The University of Wisconsin image goes back
to before World War I—the strength of Progressive and Socialist
party politics in the state contributed to its political aura. Berkeley is
a particularly interesting case in point. The San Francisco Bay area
has a history, dating back to the turn of the century, of being among
the most liberal-left communities in the nation. Various data pertain-
ing to the Berkeley campus since the end of World War II point up

the continuity of that university as a center of leftism. Berkeley was the only major institution in the country to sustain a major faculty revolt against restrictive anticommunist personnel policies in the form of the loyalty-oath controversy of 1946–50. The data collected by Paul Lazarsfeld in a national opinion survey of the attitudes of social scientists, conducted in 1954 to evaluate the effect of McCarthyism on universities, indicated that the Berkeley faculty members were the most liberal of any of the school sampled in this study. In 1963–64, the year before the celebrated Berkeley student revolt, San Francisco Bay area students received national publicity for a series of successful massive sit-in demonstrations, at various business firms, designed to secure jobs for Negroes. Prior to the emergence of the Free Speech Movement (FSM) the Berkeley campus probably had more different left-wing and activist groups with more members than any other school in the country. The vigor and effectiveness of the FSM must in some part be credited to the prior existence of a well-organized and politically experienced group of activist students. A study of the 600 students who held a police car captive in the first major confrontation of that affair in October 1964, reported that over half of them had taken part in at least one previous demonstration, and that 15 per cent indicated they had taken part in *seven or more*. Since the Berkeley revolt, Bay area activists have continued their leading role—by major efforts to disrupt the operation of the Selective Service, by conducting two of the four most publicized student demonstrations of 1967–68, and by a recent Paris-style confrontation with the Berkeley police.

In stressing that involvement in leftist student activism is a function of the general political orientation which students bring to the university, it is not being argued that changes in attitude do not occur, or even that conversions do not take place. Universities clearly do have a liberalizing effect, so that there is a gradual shift to the left. A significant number of students in the mid-1960s have been much more radical in their actions and opinions than postwar generations of American students, or than their parents. The larger events which created a basis for a renewed visible radical movement have influenced many students to the left of the orientation in which they were reared. Many students with liberal parents have felt impelled to act out the moral imperatives implicit in the seemingly "academic" liberalism of the older generation. Political events combined with various elements in the situation of students pressed a number of liberal students to become active radicals. The principal predisposing factors which determined who among the students would become activists, however, existed before they entered the university.

However, if we hold preuniversity orientation constant, it obviously will make a difference which university a student attends, what subjects he decides to major in, who his friends are on the campus, what his relations are with his teachers of varying political persuasions, what particular extracurricular activities he happens to get involved in, and the like. The relationships between the orientations which students form before university and the choices they make after entering which help maintain their general political stances are only correlations; many students necessarily behave differently from the way these relationships would predict.

Clearly, conversions, drastic changes in belief, in political identity, do occur among university students, as among other groups. During a period in which events shift the larger political climate to the left or right, young people, with fewer ties to the past, are undoubtedly more likely to change than older ones. There is also a special aspect of university life which enhances the chances that certain groups of students will be more likely to find satisfaction in intense political experience. Various studies suggest that mobility, particularly geographic mobility, where one becomes a stranger in an unfamiliar social context, is conducive to making individuals available for causes which invoke intense commitment.

Thus new students, or recent transfers, are more likely to be politically active than those who have been in the social system for longer periods. The various Berkeley studies underwrite this. Local students, or those relatively close to home, are less likely to be active than those who are a considerable distance from their home communities. In Berkeley, Madison, and other university centers, the activists have come disproportionately from the ranks of the migrants, and of recently arrived new students.

Some of the recent research by psychologists seeks to go beyond the analysis of factors which seem to have a direct impact on political choice, seeking the source of varying orientations and degrees of involvement in personality traits. Thus psychologists have studied such factors as variations in the way different groups of students have been reared by their parents—i.e., in a permissive or authoritarian atmosphere—as well as family relationships, student intelligence, sociability, and the like. Such studies have reported interesting and relatively consistent differences between the minority of student activists and the rest of the student population. At the moment, however, these findings are unconvincing, in large part because the extant studies do not hold the sociological and politically relevant factors in the backgrounds of the students constant. For example, they report that leftist activists tend to be the offspring of permissive families as judged by child-rearing practices, and of families characterized by a strong mother who dominates family life and decisions. Conversely, conservative activists tend to come from families with more strict relationships between parents and children, and in which the father plays a dominant role. To a considerable extent these differences correspond to the variations reported in studies of Jewish and Protestant families. Childhood rearing practices tend to be linked to socio-cultural-political outlooks. To prove that such factors play an independent role in determining the political choices of students, it will first be necessary to compare students *within* similar ethnic, religious, and political-cultural environments. This has not yet been done.

But if we cannot conclude that the differences in the family structures of committed leftists and rightists are causally related to the side of the spectrum which they choose, the fact that they have been reared differently should mean that they vary in their personality traits and consequent political styles. David Riesman has pointed out that conservative student activists seem to be afraid of the emotion of pity and compassion, that they find a concern for the "weak" threatening. Conversely, the leftists, more likely to have been raised in female-dominated families, are more prone to be open expressively toward "feminine" concerns. The possibility that American left-wing students come from more permissive and female-dominated families than their European counterparts may be linked to the fact that they have shown a greater impatience to wait, to take a prolonged time perspective. As yet, however, attempts to draw political conclusions from such psychological differences must be presented as informed guesses.

In evaluating the growing body of research on the characteristics of leftist activists by psychologists, it is also important to note whether they are being compared with other activists or, as often is done, with data from the bulk of the student population, that is, largely the passive majority. Leftist activists should be compared with conservative activists, and with those involved in nonpolitical forms of campus activity. The limited efforts in these directions indicate that some of the characteristics which have been identified as those of leftist activists, such as greater intelligence, characterize the involved generally. Both leftist and conservative activists, as well as moderates involved in student government, are drawn from the ranks of the academically talented in the United States.

Efforts to distinguish among the social and psychological traits of students of different persuasions which concentrate primarily on activists also present special analytical problems inherent in the fact that whether or not students direct their extracurricular energies into politics is strongly linked to political orientations. Studies of student bodies in different countries indicate that those on the left generally (and the small group on the extreme right) view politics as an appropriate and even necessary university activity. Committed morally to the need for major social changes, leftists feel that the university should be an agency for social change, that both they and their professors should devote a considerable portion of their activities to politics.

Conversely, however, the less leftist students are, the more likely they are to disagree with this view, the more prone they will be to feel that the university should be an apolitical "house of study." Liberals and leftists, therefore, are much more likely to be politically active than moderates and conservatives. A relatively strong conservative stance will not be reflected in membership or activity in a conservative political club. This means that on any given campus or in any country, the visible forms of student politics will suggest that the student population as a whole is more liberal or radical leftist than it actually is. Since conservative academic ideology fosters campus political passivity, one should not expect to find much conservative activity.

Presumably it takes a lower threshold of political interest or concern to activate a liberal or leftist than a conservative. One would deduce, therefore, that the average conservative student activist should be more of an extremist within his ideological tendency than the average liberal. Hence a comparison of campus activities of different persuasions should contain a greater share of extremists among the conservatives than among the liberals.

No society should find it remarkable that a visible proportion of its student population is actively involved in politics. It can be strongly argued that the circumstances of their being a "privileged" group which gives them the psychic security to act are also among the factors which make their activism possible. It can also be argued on the same grounds that a politically inactive student population is a cause for greater misgivings than is an active one. There is also the danger, however, that the indiscriminate use of violence and disruption by students and others may result in the undermining of the role of law and encouragement to all groups (including the military) to take the law and general power into their own hands whenever they feel politically frustrated.

IN DEFENSE OF STUDENT RADICALS

Jack Newfield

When did it all begin? Was it the Youth March for Integrated Schools in April of 1959, when 20,000 members of the Silent Generation unexpectedly assembled in the shadow of the Lincoln Memorial? Was it the first student lunchcounter sit-in at Greensboro, North Carolina on February 1, 1960? Was it the student demonstrations against the House Un-American Activities Committee in Berkeley three months later? Or was it the publication of C. Wright Mills' prophetic "Letter to the New Left" in October of 1960? Or was it the election of John Kennedy as President that really generated the fertile climate for concentration? Or was it the visionary monologues of Lenny Bruce, or the example of Castro's triumph in Cuba, or the founding of Students for a Democratic Society (SDS) by Tom Hayden and Al Haber?

No matter. Something called the New Left exists, will soon be one decade old, and is still growing. The January 1969 issue of business-oriented *Fortune* magazine published the results of an in-depth survey of young people between the ages of eighteen and twenty-four. The study indicated that about 750,000 of the nation's 6.7 million college students now "identify with the New Left," and that two-fifths of that group—about 3 million—"are defined . . . mainly by their lack of concern about making money." And this study neglected movement alumni over twenty-five, and ignored the volatile high-school constituency, which in urban centers is probably even more alienated and rebellious than the university students. As a writer for the *Berkeley Barb* recently put it, "The high schools are uncontainable. Che Guevara is thirteen years old, and he is not doing his homework."

With the *New York Times* reporting new high-school and college insurgencies every day, and a national backlash of paranoia developing about Student Militants, it is time, I suspect, for an accounting of this badly misreported and misunderstood mood and movement.

1. *The New Left is real.* It can't be comfortably dismissed as merely the involuntary Freudian revolt against fathers, or as the infantile equivalent of panty raids, or as the manipulated conspiracy of Maoist cadres. The activists generally come from liberal, middle- and upper-class families, and tend to be the brightest and most sensitive members of their generation. This fact has been documented in studies by Yale psychologist Kenneth Keniston, and published in his book, *Young Radicals* (Harcourt, Brace & World, Inc.). The Cox Commission Report on the student movement at Columbia University concluded that "the present generation of young people in our universities is the best informed, the most intelligent, and the most sensitive to public issues." And the late Robert Kennedy wrote in his book, *To Seek a Newer World:*

> Not since the founding of the Republic . . . has there been a younger generation of Americans brighter, better educated, or more highly motivated than this one. In the Peace Corps, in the Northern Student Movement, in Appalachia, on dusty roads in Mississippi and narrow trails in the Andes, this generation of young people has shown an idealism and a devotion to country matched in few nations and excelled in none.[1]

The Cox Commission, Dr. Keniston, and Senator Kennedy had in mind the typical, restive, morally concerned activist. They were not talking about the lunatic fringe that practices violence, arson, or terrorism—and neither am I. Part of the problem in understanding the young radicals is that the mass media have perceived no legitimate political or historical space between Eugene McCarthy and Mark Rudd—between voting and violence. The media—the networks and the weekly news magazines in particular—have painted a tyrannizing caricature of the Student Rioter. He has long, dirty hair,

[1] Robert F. Kennedy, *To Seek a Newer World* (Garden City, N.Y.: Doubleday & Company, Inc., 1967), p. 1—Eds.

an insatiable libido, and a vocabulary plagiarized from *Portnoy's Complaint*. He is violent, irrational and antidemocratic. He is humorless and hates America.

But this caricature actually fits only the few activists who are revolutionaries. There are only about 30,000 SDS members—out of an alienated youth constituency of 3 million—and not everyone in SDS endorses violence. The caricature, created by the needs and biases of the mass media, fails to take into account all the creative, extraparliamentary—*but nonviolent*—movements and programs young activists participate in.

Some specifics. There is grudging, undramatic community organizing going on every day. Attempts at mobilizing peaceful resistance to the Vietnam war are taking place within the Army itself. New institutions like high-school student unions, free universities, and underground newspapers are being built. Books and articles about community control, women's liberation, rock music, and imperialism are being written. Demonstrations are being organized against university complicity with the military establishment, against repression of dissent, and for more black students and faculty, and for an end to the endless war in Vietnam. These demonstrations are certainly less violent than the union strikes and sit-downs of the 1930s, and seem to me a legitimate part of democratic process. They are the only countervailing pressure available to students and poor people against an Establishment that can hire professional press agents and lobbyists, plant sympathetic magazine stories, take newspaper ads, make large financial contributions to political candidates, and in general use their position and wealth to get their point of view across between elections.

Perhaps the most distinctive quality of the student movement is that its politics are existential—open-ended, invented spontaneously in direct action, mistrustful of dogma, and responsive to intuitive passions. Most young radicals, at this transitional juncture in time, seem to feel no abiding allegiance to any existing national leader, party, or organization. Their style is freelance and *ad hoc*. Many of the same students who burned their draft cards in 1967 shaved their beards to work inside the system for Eugene McCarthy in 1968. After they were beaten by the Chicago police, and saw Humphrey nominated even though he won not a single presidential primary, they voted for Eldridge Cleaver for President. But now many work in support of the grapepickers' strike, led by the last, best apostle of nonviolence, Cesar Chavez.

They are neither reformers nor revolutionaries. They are just as likely to follow Tom Hayden as Teddy Kennedy in 1972. Their values are still changing, and their minds are still open. No caricature can enclose them.

2. *There are significant evils in American society that should be actively protested—war, poverty, racism, and violence.* Since the Vietnam war was expanded and Americanized by Lyndon Johnson, there have been 33,000 Americans killed, approximately a million dead Vietnamese, and more than 2 million homeless Vietnamese refugees. The government we support in Saigon is as corrupt and antidemocratic as ever. And the endless, criminal war goes on, and on, and on.

Between 32 and 40 million Americans are excluded from the affluent society. They see the taunting trophies of abundance on television, and in store windows each day, while they live in poverty, and sometimes hunger. This impoverished minority includes the aged and disabled; poor whites in Appalachia; Indians living on reservations; migrant farm laborers; and millions of blacks caged in urban ghettoes. And as the Kerner Commission Report stated, in isolating "white racism" as the root cause of five summers of disorders:

> What white Americans have never fully understood—but what the Negro can never forget—is that white society is deeply implicated in the ghetto. White institutions created it, white institutions maintain it, and white society condones it.[2]

Students and blacks—and their national spokesmen—are overwhelmingly the victims rather than the perpetrators of violence. More than one hundred young people—mostly partisans of Eugene McCarthy—were hospitalized as a result of the "police riot" during

[2] *Report of the National Advisory Commission on Civil Disorders* (New York: Bantam Books, 1968), p. 2—Eds.

the Democratic Convention in Chicago last August. Dozens of students were injured when police broke up the Columbia sit-in in spring of '68. (Both the Walker Report[3] and the Cox Commission Report[4] criticized excessive police violence in those two situations.) Three black college students were killed—shot in the back—by State troopers at Orangeburg, South Carolina last year. Black Panther leader Bobby Hutton was killed by Oakland police last April after he walked out of a building with his hands held above his head. And the very best who have sought to reform the system from within— John Kennedy, Medgar Evers, Martin Luther King, and Robert Kennedy—have all been assassinated. In addition, this generation has grown up watching its own government kill a million people to gain its goals in Vietnam. As one high-school activist recently said to me, "Man, I'm not extremist. The government is extremist."

One of the clearest examples of the Establishment's double standard about the use of violence came in the pamphlet, "Concerning Dissent and Civil Disobedience" by former Justice Abe Fortas. At one point he lectures students protesting the war that, "violent activities, in my judgment, should be regarded and treated as intolerable." But a few pages later, he says of the American police action in Korea, "It cost us over 150,000 casualties. . . . But I think it is a fairly universal opinion in the Western World that the war was a necessary action."

Is it any wonder, then, that Rap Brown can say that "violence is as American as cherry pie"?

3. *The university is implicated in all these evils, particularly with the military–scientific–industrial complex.* The American university is not a disinterested community of scholars. It offers courses for credit in ROTC training. It conducts secret chemical, biological,

---

[3] The *Walker Report* is the report to the National Commission on the Causes and Prevention of Violence concerning the events surrounding the 1968 Democratic Convention in Chicago. *Rights in Conflict* (New York, N.Y.: E. P. Dutton and Co., Inc., 1968)—Eds.

[4] The *Cox Commission Report* is the report of the Fact-Finding Commission Appointed to Investigate the Disturbances at Columbia University in April and May, 1968. *Crisis at Columbia: A Report* (New York, N.Y.: Vintage Books, 1968)—Eds.

and germ warfare research. It has covert relations with the CIA. It cooperates with draft boards and the FBI. It permits student recruiting by the Marines and Dow Chemical, the major manufacturer of napalm. According to James Ridgeway's superb book, *The Closed Corporation,* two-thirds of all university research funds come from the Defense Department, the Atomic Energy Commission, and NASA. MIT and Johns Hopkins run centers which design missiles. The Dean of Students at Princeton and the former Treasurer of Yale were CIA recruiters. The University of Michigan was subsidized by the government to conduct secret studies in counterinsurgency. Columbia University conducted research projects secretly funded by the CIA.

Until students exposed these covert institutional arrangements, the university administrators flatly denied their existence. This was specifically true at Columbia University, where both former President Grayson Kirk and Acting President Andrew Cordier, in 1967, issued false disclaimers to both faculty members and to the *Spectator,* the student newspaper. The Cox Commission, which probed the student disorders at Columbia, concluded:

> Although both President Kirk and Dean [now President] Cordier may well have sincerely believed that their statements were accurate, their remarks impaired confidence in the Administration, both at that time (1967) and through constant repetition.[5]

4. *The history of the last eight years vindicates the actions and analysis of the New Left much more than it does the behavior of the Democratic Party liberals.* It was not the stylish Kennedy Administration, but college students—black and white—who first drew attention to the racism and violence in the South. It was SNCC, and the Freedom Riders, and the martyred Goodman, Chaney, and Schwerner, not a benevolent federal bureaucracy, that first stirred the national conscience enough to pass two civil rights bills.

It was SDS and a few professors who began the opposition movement to the Vietnam war in April of 1965, while Richard Goodwin, Bill Moyers, and Hubert Humphrey were still working in LBJ's White House. It was the Northern Student Movement and SDS that

[5] *Ibid.,* p. 92—Eds.

first drew attention to the sickness of the cities, five years before the Kerner Commission Report was released. It was the students of the Free Speech Movement, in Berkeley in 1964, who first challenged the computerized authority of the soulless multiversity, while Clark Kerr and Governor Brown insisted there was no problem. It was students who began to work in the "Dump Johnson" movement, and later the McCarthy and Kennedy campaigns, while the unions and the old-line Negro leaders like Bayard Rustin supported Lyndon Johnson, and then Hubert Humphrey. And while young people were struggling to start dozens of underground newspapers across the country, it was revealed that [the British journal] *Encounter* had received a secret stipend from the CIA. To a whole new generation, official liberalism has come to be symbolized by Hubert Humphrey embracing Mayor Daley, Lyndon Johnson embracing General Ky, and university presidents embracing the National Guard.

What is happening now is *not* that the country is becoming more conservative, but that *liberalism is becoming more conservative.*

5. *The roots of the student disaffection are cultural rather than political.* What is most radical and self-liberating about the activists is their rejection of the most basic middle-class values of American society. Money and material wealth, as the *Fortune* magazine survey indicated, are unimportant to them. Equally unimportant are conventional definitions of patriotism, religion, Puritanism, and status. They desire a totally new life style and new career options. They don't want a meaningless 9-to-5 corporate job, or to live out lives of quiet desperation in split-level suburbia. They don't want to be bright young men writing memos in federal agencies. And it is this break with traditional majority culture that makes political protest like draft resistance and community organizing so accessible.

What the activists are doing is trying to create a new, adversary culture, based on life style and psychic liberation. Drugs, rock music, underground papers, long hair, communes, colorful dress, and liberated sex are all part of it. Some of the vessels of these new values are Dylan's songs, Marcuse's books, Godard's films, Mailer's journalism, and Ginsberg's life style.

At the center of this cultural insurgency, I think, is the perception that adult society is literally absurd, that America is threatening to become a giant lunatic asylum. Some recent Orwellian examples: thousands of Americans have died in Vietnam while their government debated the shape of a table in Paris; the American government can send 20,000 Marines to the Dominican Republic because there are fifty-seven communists there, but it can't send eighty-two Federal voting registrars to Mississippi, where there are still thousands of unregistered Negroes; the President can welcome the Senate's passage of the Nuclear Non-proliferation Treaty one day, and the very next day announce America will build a nuclear antiballistic-missile system (ABM); the young have literally grown up absurd, listening to Eichmann, CIA recruiters, Richard Speck, Jack Ruby, and Dean Rusk.

And so it is quite natural that the young should draw their ethic and sensibility primarily from the artist of the absurd. From the songs of Dylan, the Beatles, the Mothers of Invention, and Phil Ochs. From novelists like Joseph Heller, Thomas Pynchon, Ken Kesey, and Terry Southern. From films like *Morgan, Dr. Strangelove,* and *A Hard Day's Night.*

It is a symptom of just how badly the student generation is misunderstood that George Kennen, in his book *Democracy and the Student Left,* can lecture the young on their "inability to see and enjoy the element of absurdity in human behavior."

Such a comment by an otherwise sensible historian and diplomat is just another reason why the activists so often feel like characters in Kesey's novel, *One Flew Over the Cuckoo's Nest,* where the inmates of the mental hospital are saner than the guards. They simply don't want to participate in a culture that kills a million Vietnamese, attempts to put Benjamin Spock and Mohammed Ali in jail for opposing that slaughter, and then places Ronald Reagan and Lester Maddox in positions of authority over their lives.

6. *There are some ideas, tactics, and fashions on the margins of the activist movement that I find morally insupportable and politically counterproductive.* Among a small minority of the student activists there is a romantic view of violence and revolution derived from a misreading of Fanon, Che, Debray, and Mao. I am

among those who happen to believe that Che Guevara might have been a second Jesus Christ for Latin America. But I don't think anything he or the others wrote is applicable to a nuclear, technological octopus like the United States. Given the government's monopoly of violence, and the prosperity of a majority of Americans, I think the idea of violent revolution here is a fantasy. Therefore I believe that resistance to the war should remain strictly nonviolent. I agree with Noam Chomsky when he writes in his new book, *American Power and the New Mandarins:*

> If there will be a "revolution" in America today, it will no doubt be a movement towards some variety of fascism. We must guard against the kind of revolutionary rhetoric that would have had Karl Marx burn down the British Museum because it was merely a part of a repressive society. It would be criminal to overlook the serious flaws and inadequacies in our institutions, or to fail to utilize the substantial degree of freedom that most of us enjoy, within the framework of these institutions, to modify them or even replace them by a better social order. One who pays some attention to history will not be surprised if those who cry most loudly that we must smash and destroy, are later found among the administrators of some new system of repression.[6]

Or, as Marcus Raskin asks, "What do you do with the gunman *after* the revolution?"

So I am opposed to assassinations, blowing up troop trains, arson, sabotage, or knocking disagreeable speakers off platforms. But it is also necessary to understand that sit-ins, picket lines, boycotts, or the physical occupation of property is *not violence*. Those tactics are in the classic and noble tradition of Tom Paine, Thoreau, Gandhi, Martin Luther King, Cesar Chavez, Danilo Dolci—and even Walter Reuther thirty years ago. *Violence* is dropping napalm on civilians or clubbing an unarmed sixteen-year-old demonstrator into unconsciousness.

Also, some of the activists don't seem to realize who their real

[6] Noam Chomsky, *American Power and the New Mandarins* (New York, N.Y.: Pantheon Books, Inc., 1969), pp. 17–18—Eds.

enemy is. In New York public speeches by maverick journalist I. F. Stone and Paul O'Dwyer have been disrupted by the Yippies. But Stone and O'Dwyer were critics of the Vietnam war from the start. They are not the enemy. The enemy is the banks and absentee landlords who own Harlem; the warrier caste in the Pentagon and the State Department; the AFL-CIO Bureaucracy; and the FBI. The enemy is institutions.

Some of the activists think that liberalism is the *primary* enemy because liberals have been in power since 1960, and have been directly responsible for the Bay of Pigs, Vietnam, the fraud the War on Poverty turned out to be, and the police riot in Chicago. But it has been *other liberals* who were the first to realize the students were right on so many issues. Liberalism is not monolithic. Both George Orwell and George Meany are liberals. It is necessary to distinguish, in Eldridge Cleaver's phrase, who is part of the *problem,* and who is part of the *solution.* It seems to me obvious that Melvin Laird is part of the problem, and I. F. Stone part of the solution. We should keep in mind that while some liberals like John Kennedy, Hubert Humphrey, and McGeorge Bundy bear much of the guilt for Vietnam, other liberals, like Robert Kennedy, Eugene McCarthy, and George McGovern, tried to stop the war. And it has been conservatives like Senator Strom Thurmond, Ronald Reagan, and Governor Connally who have always wanted to escalate it.

All this said, I would still maintain that, on balance, the young Left—from McCarthy volunteers to draft resisters—is more worthy of support than any competing movement, including the hippie dropouts, the older NATO liberals, or the operatives of the New Politics, who have no vision beyond the 1972 elections.

7. *The student protest movement is now in serious danger of re-pression by the Nixon Administration.* America is not likely to give birth to another generation so humanistic and generous in its im-pulses as this one for many years. This is a generation that values people above things, and that has jeopardized its own safe careers to save a small nation 10,000 miles away from the fate of genocide. They have been called cowards for refusing the draft, but thousands risked their lives to register black voters in the South. This is a

generation that has witnessed its most respected adult sympathizers assassinated in a systematic horror show, but still refuses to withdraw into a painless privatism.

But now there is the possibility that the best of this generation will be jailed, or driven underground, in a paranoid paroxysm of repression.

Eight New Left leaders have been indicted in Chicago for the demonstrations that took place during the Democratic convention, although if the grand jury had bothered to read the Walker Report they would have indicted Chicago's Mayor Daley instead. The Justice Department is supporting preventive detention and increased wire tapping. President Nixon has put out an antistudent statement,[7] and every state legislature in the country has been flooded with antistudent bills.[8] A Long Island judge sentenced thirty-one students from Stony Brook College of New York to fifteen days in jail and called them "animals" for a nonviolent sit-in. Tom Hayden is followed twenty-four hours a day, his phone is tapped, and his mail is opened. Eldridge Cleaver is in exile. Rap Brown is free only on bail. The first foul odors of a new McCarthyism are in the air. And many liberals seem willing to quietly pay the ransom of a little repression to buy some tranquility and time. Just like the 1950s, when intellectuals like Sidney Hook saw no problem with Senator McCarthy, as long as he left their friends alone.

My reflex is to end with an inspirational quote from Tom Paine or Jefferson. Or an optimistic summons to some barricade. But that would be too easy, and unfaithful to my mood most of the time these days.

Things are getting worse, not better. Nixon's decisions on the ABM[9] and the Chicago indictments prove that our darkest suspicions about him may have been generous.

[7] President Nixon's speech of June 3rd, 1969, at General Beadle State College in Madison, South Dakota. "Nixon Says Rebels Imperil Education," *The Washington Post* (June 4, 1969), Sec. A, p. 1—Eds.

[8] How various states are attempting to prevent campus unrest is discussed in the article "Many States Enacting Laws to Curb Campus Disorders," *The Washington Post* (June 2, 1969), Sec. A, p. 3—Eds.

[9] On March 14, 1969, President Nixon announced at a Press Conference that plans would proceed for the creation of an antiballistic missile system—Eds.

What I want to say in conclusion is simple and blunt. The student activists are the best young this nation will produce for a generation. They are right on most specific issues. The government, the courts, the police, and the college administrations may finally have the institutional power to forcefully repress this beginning movement. But if that happens, America will become a poorer and meaner country.

THE UNIVERSITY AND REVOLUTION:
A QUESTION OF RELEVANCE

Samuel L. Sharp

A brilliant observer and critic of the American scene, H. L. Mencken, long ago predicted a time when every American citizen will receive his bachelor's degree as part of his birthright. We may be heading in just that direction. The whole business of higher education will then wither away or, to borrow further from Marx and Engels, will be thrown on the scrapheap of history as so much useless rubbish. In anticipation of this glorious day, some of us who are making a living in this field are secretly taking courses to qualify as maintenance and repair men of the computers which will fully replace the no longer needed, irrelevant teachers.

But let us talk about "relevance," which, as used in certain circles, is actually an abbreviation for "irrelevance" (a word simply too long for the current postverbal generation that, like its contemporary the computer, refuses to handle words of more than seven letters and, in fact, sees no need for anything that has more than four). What is relevance and in what way can a university be relevant? And who is competent to judge what is relevant? And, by the way, relevant to what?

A complex and sophisticated society must be based on some form of division of labor and assignment of roles. The relevant role (I hate the word *mission*) of a university is to teach; it is in this way and in this way only that a university knows how to be relevant and make its contribution to the larger community. The direct connection between what a university teaches and what is relevant to the problems of the larger community may not be visible to the naked and untrained eye. As William Shannon of the *New York Times* recently put it, "A university serves its community and its nation in roundabout and even mysterious ways." Those on the receiving end must try to trust those who map out educational programs; they must assume, so to say, on credit that what may appear irrelevant or boring at the time when it is being forced down one's throat may somehow turn out to be relevant at some later date. Generation gap or no generation gap, there must be some things which a younger generation will take from an older one on trust; otherwise every generation would have to start from the beginning, invent the wheel and the table of multiplication and a number of other things which even the younger birds and bees learn from the older birds and bees though it possibly puzzles them at first.

Let me give you a very simple example of the need to assume relevance. My daughter refused to see the relevance of my advice when I counseled her as a seventh-grader to take Latin. Now, a number of years later, she finds herself handicapped as applicant for graduate study of comparative literature at Yale by requirement number one: Latin. This shows that education in Latin is at least relevant to further education; but this is a lot.

It may well be that the universities deserve some of the trouble they are now facing. I have never been too happy with the image of their role and the description of their capabilities which many American educational institutions tended to create (possibly in response to the tolerance for overstatement which our advertising culture encourages or out of a guilt feeling connected with the high cost of education). Parents who plunked down the prescribed amounts were promised, directly or by implication, that they have secured for their offspring a combination babysitter, chastity-watcher, matchmaker, and provider of glamorous jobs. Education was advertised just like deodorants, with the usual threats of dire consequences if you didn't and blessed results if you did. Now this was simply too much to promise and a wasteful input and dispersal of energies. I sometimes dream of a courageous inscription on the main gate: "We do NOT educate the whole child, we merely teach." Our come-on literature should say over and over again: We teach and that is all. In fact, we decline responsibility for what you will do with your knowledge although we hope for the best. A professor

of toxicology has no guarantee that the knowledge he imparted to a
student will be used to produce safe drugs rather than to poison
his mother-in-law. Education is a big and exciting gamble. Not every
participant in the game can win. But a university can preserve its
relevance only by sticking to its assigned societal role. Otherwise
it will be transformed into a totalitarian mishmash.

To the suggestion that the younger generation must take some
things on trust one hears the frequent answer that the generation
claiming to be able to teach them has not really done much to earn
their confidence. This is a serious point and it cannot be lightly
dismissed. We indeed have much to account for. With all our
frantic efforts propelled by the ethic of hard work and good deeds,
why have we managed to spread or perpetuate so much misery and
injustice? Why has our devotion to technological progress produced
the monstrous capacity to destroy life itself on this planet? There is
not much to excuse all this except perhaps to admit humbly that
every generation is caught in its own chapter of the human predica-
ment, in the as-yet-unresolved struggle between man's primitive
biological heritage and his claim to be not just an updated dinosaur,
but a rational being, whether created in God's image or capable of
creating the image of gods.

The educational system, along with other societal institutions, can
respond relevantly to the challenging questions of *some* young
people (though there is not much one can say to or do for those
whom Bruno Bettelheim calls spoiled brats incapable of outgrowing
the habit of throwing temper tantrums). The honest contribution of
education, especially of higher as against merely longer education,
would consist of attempts to curb the temptation to be self-congratu-
latory and self-indulgent, to forego the ridiculous effort to preach
down to a very smart and sensitive generation, to give up the confidence game of proclaiming stable values in the shadow of the
thermonuclear umbrella—or putting it simply, to let out some of
the hot air with which each mature generation seems to fill itself.
We must not describe in rapturous terms the golden garments of
the king when his majesty is actually naked or parades around in
bloodstained or napalm-soaked rags. We must not think of our role
as interference runners for God and country. God—thank God—

can take care of himself, even in Argentina; and the country, or those who run it, could use a second look, and a critical one.

The university will have fulfilled its duty to you, if within the framework of its relevant role in a pluralistic and complex society, it has taught you to doubt; yes: to doubt, to doubt what to the semi-educated and the totally unwashed seems self-evident. It is *not* the function of the university to shore up the prejudices which you brought here from home, street, mass media, and other segments of the larger community. Your civic loyalties should have been taken care of in grammar school (also your grammar): your surface knowledge of things, familiarity with people and places, the entire caboodle of facts and figures which is of help in solving crossword puzzles, should have been conveyed to you in secondary school. The university is a place which should have instilled in you the habits of contemplation and the capacity to doubt—to doubt cre-atively—what is thrown at you from various quarters, including high ones. Higher education is a bulldozing operation, an attempt to clear away nonsense, including time-honored nonsense, to pull out by the very roots the most deeply built-in clichés and miscon-ceptions. To the extent that the university carries out this function, which to some appears subversive—and it is indeed subversive, subversive of what we politely call these days bull—to this extent it will have lived up in a relevant fashion to its role in society. That role is as a provider of *critical* knowledge, a role worth defending against attempts to tamper with and possibly destroy a delicate and fragile instrument not really equipped to participate directly in contests of power, of human impatience and folly, a tool designed only to record and evaluate these things critically.

I would be untrue to myself if I were to end on a note of cheap confidence that all of you have really grasped the nature of the contribution the university has made or, for that matter, that every-one garbed in academic robes has necessarily contributed his best along those lines. There is no certainty, there is no guarantee, there is only hope. It is up to you to justify this hope. It is up to us to try to play our *relevant* role better.

THE STUDENT AS WORKER

James H. Weaver

Recently in my graduate course in economic development we were discussing the course that economic development had taken in England—the viciousness of the factory system—and I had read the class three passages from Marx's *Capital* in which he described life in the typical nineteenth-century English factory.

Marx details conditions as revealed in Parliamentary inquiries of 1860 in Nottingham:

> Children of nine or ten years are dragged from their squalid beds at two, three, or four o'clock in the morning and compelled to work for a bare subsistence until ten, eleven, or twelve at night, their limbs wearing away, their frames dwindling, their faces whitening, and their humanity absolutely sinking into a stone-like torpor, utterly horrible to contemplate.[1]

And then he recounts conditions in the potteries of Staffordshire where members of Parliament found a seven-year-old child working from six in the morning until nine at night—fifteen hours of labor for a child of seven.

But, Marx reserves his greatest anger for his description of the lucifer-match factories. The problem with these factories was that the phosphorus used in the matches brought lockjaw which killed the workers. Members of Parliament found that half the workers were under thirteen and, in one factory, "50 were under ten, 10 only eight and 5 were only six years old. A range of the working day from twelve to fourteen hours, night-labor, irregular meal times, meals for the most part taken in the very workrooms that are filled

---

[1] Karl Marx, *Capital*, Vol. I (New York: Random House, 1906), 268.

with phosphorus." Marx adds that "Dante would have found the worst horrors of his Inferno surpassed in this manufacture."

Tears were running down the cheeks of the students in the class when one of them—a young man from Trinidad—said, "Don't the schools play that same role today?"

I had to think about it, but it seems that he is right—the modern equivalent of the nineteenth-century factory is the schoolroom. During the nineteenth century, the system needed illiterate people who could run simple machinery, carry heavy loads, do piecework for long hours at rapid speeds—and what better way of teaching these skills than to put children into the factories at an early age? There they could be disciplined to sit still many hours, work rapidly, carry heavy loads, etc. By doing this from age six, they would learn to accept it as the natural lot of man. They would be acculturated to their lot in life.

Adam Smith understood this perfectly and described the process in quite forceful terms:

> The man whose whole life is spent in performing a few simple operations, of which the effects too are, perhaps, always the same, or very nearly the same, has no occasion to exert his understanding, or to exercise his invention in finding out expedients for removing difficulties which never occur. He naturally loses, therefore, the habit of such exertion, and generally becomes as stupid and ignorant as it is possible for a human creature to become. . . . But in every improved and civilized society this is the state into which the labouring poor, that is, the great body of the people, must necessarily fall.[2]

Today we have lost Smith's honesty in admitting that, in an industrial society, the great body of the people must perform tasks which cause them to become "as stupid and ignorant as it is possible for a human creature to become." But, even if we do not admit it, we have devised a perfect institution for reducing people to the state required by the system—and this institution is the school (the education factory).

[2] Adam Smith, *The Wealth of Nations* (New York: Random House, Inc., 1937), pp. 734-35.

Technology has almost eliminated the need for illiterate people who can do simple tasks. We have virtually no demand today for box-kickers and label-lickers. What we do need is people who are literate, enured to boredom, able to take orders, do fairly complicated mathematics, etc. The factory is not an efficient place for training people for these tasks. The school is.

This fact was brought home very clearly when I recently visited a first-grade classroom on visitor's day. The children sit at nice little desks in neat little lines—much like the desks in government offices or large corporations. They are told what to do by an authority figure who puts them neatly through their tricks. They march around the room when she tells them to march around the room. They sit down when she tells them to sit down. They are quiet when she tells them to be quiet. When their group is not reading, they sit and color—in nice straight lines that the teacher has put on the paper, and she grades them on how well they have followed directions—how neatly they have colored, how well they stayed within the lines.

The reading book they use is *Dick and Jane*, and it describes nice middle-class kids in a nice middle-class environment—a family with a nice house, a nice car, a nice television set, a nice green lawn—that is America.

They happened to be learning about the first Thanksgiving, and they were learning how nice the Pilgrims were to the Indians—they invited them to come and share the feast and the Indians stayed three days. No mention was made of the fact that the Pilgrims seized the Indians' land and finally wound up killing the Indians.

During the afternoon they went out on the athletic field and sang martial songs in observance of Veteran's Day. They went home singing "From the Halls of Montezuma to the Shores of Tripoli" and "Over hill, over dale, we will hit the dusty trail, as those caissons go rolling along." Militarism is an important part of American society and, therefore, we need to start inculcating these values at an early age.

In elementary school, they are taught how to write simple sentences, how to read well enough to follow written instructions, and how to do simple mathematics. However, one of the most important lessons learned in elementary school is to compete. Everyone is in competition with everyone else to get the teacher's approval—to get the best grade—and each child is vigorously competing with everyone else in the class—striving for those limited numbers of A's which will be handed out. So, the most important lesson learned in elementary school is how to compete.

In high school, we begin the process of sorting out the workers. Some will go to college and get additional training for management positions. They are put in the college-preparatory track and they dare not descend into the basement where the vocational-education program is going on, for fear of loss of limb or even life.

Below the college-preparatory track we have the business-education track. Here the training involves accounting, typing, business English, business math, etc. These people may go on to junior college and learn to be foremen. Or they may go out into the other factory and begin their work immediately.

Below the business-education track we have the vocational-educational program. This program teaches people to fix cars, paint, do carpentry, etc. There is no pretense made to teach literature or music or art. In order to make it perfectly clear that the school is preparation for the factory, the trainees in the vocational education program often spend a considerable part of their day in actual factories.

Colleges and universities are the plush factories for those workers who are selected to go into the higher posts in the American factory system. The colleges and universities are ranked hierarchically. The sons and daughters of the power elite go to Harvard, Yale, Princeton, Vassar, Radcliffe, Smith and there are fitted for places in the establishment. Some very able and adept young people from the lower strata are also admitted into these institutions so that they can be hired to help manage the American factory system.

The less prestigious schools are designed for those people who are scheduled for the middle-management jobs or the less prestigious professional jobs.

The junior colleges, community colleges, and vocational or technical institutes are designed for those workers who will fill foremen positions and white-collar jobs in the other factory.

Colleges and universities continue the emphasis on competition. Grades are again all-important and athletics are central. Competition is the key to success in America today, and the schools are preparing the nation's workers for successful lives within the system.

Some additional skills are taught—how to run computers, how to manage the Federal budget so that capitalism is more efficient, how to carry on representative government—in an environment where the crucial issue is the choice of a Homecoming Queen. This will prepare people for voting in elections where the choice is between Nixon and Humphrey. The questions of what-will-be-taught-and-how are decided by the foremen (the faculty) in close cooperation with the management (the administration) which is, of course, appointed by the board of trustees (the absentee owners of the factory).

The fraternities and sororities teach useful social skills—how to mix drinks, how to dress fashionably, how to wear formal clothes, how to waste money in conspicuous consumption.

Of course, those workers who are fortunate enough to be in colleges are deferred from the draft. When workers come out of college, they are further divided and some—those who have demonstrated the greatest ability to compete for grades and those whose parents can afford it—go on to graduate school. These workers are also exempt from the draft and will be beyond draft age by the time they have finished their graduate and postgraduate training.

Everyone knows what the end of all this factory training is—a job in the other factory which will now give out goodies instead of grades. The more successful we are in competing, the more goodies we will get—a big house, two cars, Baccarat crystal, portraits by Bachrach, trips to Europe, etc., etc.

There is only one problem in this otherwise idyllic situation. As technology advances, the industrial machine becomes more and more complex. Thus higher levels of education are required in order to operate this complex system. And, despite its effect on most students, education does have a liberating effect on some people. There is a dispute as to whether this liberation results from scientific education (being taught to ask "Why?") and humanistic education ("What is man?" "What is a good society?") or whether the liberation occurs as the result of rebelling against the repressiveness of the educational system. Perhaps both factors are at work. In any case, there are certain disruptive elements in the education factories today.

Some workers are alienated by the machines that have been introduced into the modern university factory. They object to teaching machines, computerized registration, television courses, etc. They remind us of the Luddites and their attempts to break up the machines by throwing bricks.

Some workers are demanding a bill of rights much as the Chartists did a century ago. They object to piecework. They are tired of competing for grades and want everyone on a straight hourly-wage system—they call it a pass–fail system.

Some workers object to their living conditions and want the visiting hours increased in the dormitories or want male and female workers to be incarcerated in the same buildings. One of my female students was arrested recently in a protest demonstration and taken to the women's jail in the District of Columbia. After she was bailed out and returned to the campus, she took one look at the dormitory and said, "Take me back to jail."

Some workers are saying that the schools belong to the students— just as some Syndicalist workers' groups argued in the nineteenth century that the factories belonged to the workers.

Some workers are demanding unionization and the right to collective bargaining with the management just as the trade unionists did in the 1930s. The foremen (faculty) are caught in the middle on this point, because they are organized also and want to bargain with the management. So, they have trouble deciding (as all foremen do) whether they are workers or management.

Some workers are arguing that, if one can alter the schools (even including the high schools), one can demonstrate that it can be done, and one can then go on to alter the American Factory System.

Astute managers are co-opting the radical workers by inviting them to participate in the decision-making process. The workers who sit on boards with trustees, managers, and foremen are carefully chosen so that they will not be disruptive. The managers are adopting the ideas of scientific management which were introducd into the other factory years ago.

There are disruptive forces at work in the American education factory. But the astute managers of today will succeed in dissipating these forces just as they succeeded in dissipating the disruptive force of the Luddites, the Chartists, the Syndicalists, and the trade unionists.

Some critics argue that the American educational system has been a failure. They are wrong. Obviously the education factory of the twentieth century is less physiologically damaging than were the factories of the nineteenth century, and for that we can be thankful. None of today's students are dying from lockjaw as the result of phosphorus in the air. The psychological damage, however, is about the same. Bright-eyed and curious six-year-old children are turned into dull-eyed and apathetic eighteen-year-olds—ready to take their place in the other factory. They have learned their lessons well. They have learned to sit down and shut up, they have learned to take orders, they have learned how to compete, they have learned to endure boredom. They can, in short, fit right into the other factory. Just like the nineteenth-century factory, the twentieth-century education factory is turning out exactly what the system needs.

THE UNIVERSITY AND REVOLUTION: AN INSANE CONJUNCTION

Russell Kirk

Already the reaction is upon us. Political leaders, college presidents, and syndicated columnists join in condemnation of violence on the campus. Yesterday's fashionable prattle about revolution in the university and revolution in the United States and revolution in the world is reproved piously by those very liberals who, such a short while ago, beamed upon the ferment of the rising generation. Mr. Irving Howe, editor of *Dissent*, wanders over the face of the land reproaching the more vehement dissenters and reminding them of the delightful benefits of Social Security. One thinks of Edward Gibbon, so progressive at the commencement of the French Revolution, observing from his Swiss retreat the course of that movement; reflecting, presently, that revolutionaries kill people like Edward Gibbon; and then promptly taking another tack.

For my part, however, I do not propose to deliver another sermon about the naughtiness of ungrateful undergraduates. Whatever the silliness of revolutionary slogans and methods, one does not deal with them by mere smug remonstrance. We need to address ourselves, rather, to the real *causes* of our present discontents, in the university and in this nation; and my observations are of that character.

The principal cause of some people's revolutionary mood is the decay of community—the decadence of academic community, and the decadence of urban community. In the phrase of Miss Hannah Arendt, "The rootless are always violent." Until community is restored, certain students and considerable elements of our urban population will continue to detest the existing order.

Having been for two decades a mordant critic of what is foolishly called the higher learning in America, I confess to relishing somewhat, as Cassandra might have, the fulfillment of my predictions and the present plight of the educationist Establishment. I even own to a sneaking sympathy, after a fashion, with the campus revolutionaries. Consider, by way of illustration, the experience of Mr. John A. Hannah, president of Michigan State University, recently chosen to be director of the Federal Government's foreign-aid program.

Called to relieve the miseries of Kerala and to improve the lot of Bolivia, President Hannah delivered his farewell address to the members of his faculty on February 10, 1969. In three decades as master of Michigan State, Dr. Hannah (the doctorate honorary, conferred by his own university on the day he became its president) had built up a student body now exceeding 40,000, with expectation of 70,000, or more, before from his eyes the streams of dotage flow. . . . On the branches of his university the sun never sets: they flourish in Okinawa and in Nigeria. Doubtless President Hannah, on this day of leavetaking, felt that he deserved well of the rising generation. Certainly he knew that *he* had done well out of the education business—having risen so far when his earned degree was that of bachelor of science in poultry husbandry—and he was determined that those national institutions which had facilitated his success should not perish from the earth.

True, he was departing from Michigan State in the nick of time. Having passed the retirement age set by himself, he was in an awkward situation when certain hostile trustees of the university hinted that he might not be altogether indispensable. The Attorney General of Michigan had looked into charges that Dr. Hannah might have engaged in activities constituting "conflict of interest. . . ."

As President Hannah addressed his professors for the last time, riot police—gas masks and all—stood guard in the auditorium. Several hundred students, a discharged instructor with a bullhorn, and a number of outsiders—among these, Carl Oglesby, of Students for a Democratic Society—were chanting unpleasantly outside the

auditorium. It was found prudent to cancel the reception that had
been scheduled to follow President Hannah's speech.

"A small coterie," the masterful chickenologist told his faculty, "has
declared social revolution against America. America's universities
have been marked as the first fortress that must fall. We've been
warned of the weapons to be used and the tactics to be employed."
He exhorted his professors to resist to the last bluebook these
enemies of civilization. Then, meaning to do high deeds beside the
Potomac, he departed from their midst.

John Hannah had been a bricks-and-mortar president. His university has become an intellectual cafeteria, or rather a vocational
cafeteria, offering every serious discipline from fly-casting (for
physical-education majors) to Afro-American studies (after all, he
had been chairman of the Civil Rights Commission, even if in his
early years of office the only Negro employee of Michigan State
had been the president's own errand boy). Unceasingly he had
recruited students, qualified or unqualified, telling them and their
parents that a college graduate earns much more money in his
lifetime than does a barbarian of the outer darkness. He had offered
students the nexus of cash payment—and what else is there to a
university, after all?

Yet the gentry of the New Left remained unappreciative. One
of them, James Ridgeway, has published a book containing lively
references to Dr. Hannah: *The Closed Corporation—American
Universities in Crisis.* Here we must content ourselves with one
passage:

> From 1950 to 1958, more than $900,000 in MSU construction
> contracts went to the Vandeburg Construction Company. The
> president of this firm was Hannah's brother-in-law, who sub-
> sequently went out of business and turned up as construction
> superintendent at MSU. Hannah was quoted as saying at the
> trustees' meeting, "It's true that Vandenburg is my brother-in-
> law, but I didn't know he was employed by the university." He
> also said, "As far as I know he never did a job for this institu-
> tion. I was surprised by the figure. . . . I smell what's coming

on. This is an attempt at discrediting the university by discrediting me." [1]

Really? Or is it the Hannahs of our time who have discredited the university, and so raised up a turbulent generation of students, at once ignorant and passionate, who nevertheless sense somehow that Hannah's idea of a university is not quite John Henry Newman's idea of a university? Having established academic collectivism, having overwhelmed academic community, having severed the intellectual and moral roots of the higher learning, people like John Hannah are chagrined to discover that the proles are restless.

So if some portion of what I say hereafter bears a superficial resemblance to portions of the farewell address of John A. Hannah, I beg your pardon. The resemblance is coincidental, and my motives and principles are not those of the present administrator of the Agency for International Development. I do not mean to smite Students for a Democratic Society, Philistines though they may be, with the jawbone of an ass.

No less a public figure than Miss Joan Baez has remarked that if one desires to be a revolutionary, the campus is an unlikely place to commence; that she is disgusted with the antics of campus radicals; and that she will have no more to do with them. One wishes that certain professors might share her wisdom. But they will, eventually—they will: for revolutions devour their children, and also their fathers.

Dr. Bruno Bettelheim, the psychologist, who has had unpleasant personal experience of revolutions, says that the crowd of campus revolutionaries—the violent folk, he means—are paranoiacs, though led by shrewd ideologues intent upon personal power. Paranoiacs may belong in an institution, but that institution is not the university; ideologues have no stopping place short of heaven or hell, and so they ought not to be permitted to convert the university into a staging ground. We need to recall the principal purpose of a university. The university is not a center for the display of adolescent tempers, nor yet a fulcrum for turning society upside down. It is

---

[1] James Ridgeway, *The Closed Corporation* (New York: Ballatine Books, Inc., 1968), p. 32—Eds.

simply this: a place for the cultivation of right reason and moral imagination.

From its beginnings, the university has been a conservative power. The principal schools of Athens, particularly the Academy and the Stoa, had as their end the recovery of order in the soul and order in the commonwealth. The medieval university was intended to impart wisdom and temperance to a violent age. My own higher studies were undertaken at St. Andrews, a university founded by the inquisitor of heretical pravity in Scotland, expressly to confute the errors of Lollardry.

So it is not in the nature of a university to nurture political fanaticism and utopian designs. The professor rarely is a neoterist, and one cannot expect the university to harvest a crop of exotic flowers annually. Dr. Robert Hutchins observes, with only a little exaggeration, that few of the Great Books were written by professors. If one would be a mover and shaker in his own hour, the forum is preferable to the grove of Academe. In a small way, I have done some moving and shaking myself; but I found myself much freer and more effective once I had withdrawn from the shadow of the Ivory Tower.

Only in our century, indeed, has the plague of ideological passion descended upon the quadrangle and the campus. To some degree, in previous times, all universities ordinarily were, after the fashion of Oxford, sanctuaries of lost causes: conservative to a fault, if you will. So far as they aspired to influence the bustling world, it was to tug at the checkrein, not to use the spur. Of ungoverned will and appetite, the average sensual man in the civil social order needs no larger endowment. The university tried to teach the rising generation how to rise superior to will and appetite.

Yet temporarily, at least, throughout the world, many a campus has fallen into the clutch of ideology, ours being a time of ideological infatuation. What the university used to offer was freedom; what some zealots seek there, just now, is power. Freedom and power are in eternal opposition. To demand that the university devote itself to the *libido dominandi* is to demand that the university commit intellectual and moral suicide.

A good many entering freshmen tell me that they desire to be

on a campus "where the action is." But of action, we all have plenty
in the course of life. A university is a place not for action, but for
leisure—that is, for reading, for good talk, for dialogue between
scholar and student, for a reflective preparation. Few people ever
find again, after they enter upon the hurly-burly of the world, time
enough to study and to think. The four or five or seven years of
college and university life are precious, then; they are a period of
self-discipline and self-examination; and, as Socrates put it, the un-
examined life is not worth living.

Even a young person who aspires to turn the civil social order
inside out is foolish if he occupies his university years in "activism."
Marching, demonstrating, shouting, sitting-in, he squanders the
time he might have used to prepare himself for effective action after
graduation. He could have been a member of an academic community; instead, he has chosen to become a face in an academic
mob; and in later years, intellectually undisciplined, he must be
virtually worthless as a partisan of radical reform. The systematic
Marxist, incidentally, is well aware of this difficulty; and though he
may make use of the anarchic student for the immediate purposes
of his movement, mere perpetual activism scarcely is the course
he commends to the initiates of a Marxist study group. The labors
of Marx were accomplished in the British Museum, not in Trafalgar
Square.

All this said, nevertheless I think I apprehend the causes of the
"New Left" mentality on the campus, and in part sympathize with
the mood of rebellion. For two decades, I have been declaring
that most colleges and universities are sunk in decadence. Against
that decadence, the confused outcries of the New Left people are
a reaction. For a university, as for the human body, the power of
reaction is a necessity, and often a sign of latent health: the body
that no longer can react is a corpse.

Against what does the radical student rebel? Against a crass and
boring and "oppressive" society, he declares; but more immediately,
he rebels against what James Ridgeway calls "the closed corporation": the university that has decayed into a vast impersonal computer, serving big government and big industry, neglecting wisdom
for isolated facts and skills, routinely conferring degrees that are

mere certificates of introduction or employability, at best; the university that has forgotten quality in the appetite for quantity, that exalts "service"—which is to say, the gratification of the whims and material desires of the hour—above learning; the university that has made some professors affluent, and some administrators more than affluent, but which leaves the typical undergraduate intellectually and morally impoverished.

Were I to indulge my taste for Jeremiads, indeed I might succeed in out-lamenting the New Left people at the Ivory Tower's wailing wall. Though they might not use precisely these words, in effect the New Left zealots are proclaiming that today's university offers next to nothing for mind and conscience. Amen to that. I am not sorry that the radicals have fluttered academic hencoops like Dr. Hannah's, for I have long been endeavoring to do precisely that myself.

What I do regret is the proclivity of the New Left to pull down. Demolition is simple enough; but the craft of the architect is something else. The university, and the modern world, require the torch: not the arsonist's torch, however, but the torch of learning. "Revolution" means violent and catastrophic change. Of catastrophe, we have experience enough already in this century. Revolution— political and technological and moral and demographic—is upon us in this century, whether we like it or not; we have no need to flog the galloping horses of the four spectres of the Apocalypse. Reconstruction, renewal, reinvigoration are the real necessities of this hour; we require creative imagination—which the university is supposed to cultivate—not the sapper's petard, that so frequently hoists its pioneer.

Our present discontents in the Academy, I repeat, are not difficult to describe. Foremost among their practical causes is the problem of scale. Behemoth University is too big; it has been inundated by, or has lured in, an academic crowd; and a crowd easily is converted into a mob. When community dies, collectivism succeeds, in the university or in the state. No man rejoices at finding himself an IBM number merely. At the institution where I spent my undergraduate years—Michigan State—a great many new graduates complain that they cannot obtain job recommendations from any professor, because they never have met a real professor, in four years of course-taking: their converse was not with Mark Hopkins, but (at best) with an obscure teaching assistant, who meanwhile has proceeded to greener pastures. At the early medieval universities, the student was an acolyte; now he has become a cipher.

Nowadays the typical student is bored. Mankind can endure anything but boredom. It is by boredom, actually, that the student is oppressed—not by "the administration" or "the establishment." Revolution always is attractive to the man intensely bored: anything for a change. But of revolution inspired by boredom, one must say what Bierce said of suicide: a door out of the prison house of life. It opens upon the jailyard. Undoubtedly the domination of King Log was boring. Yet as for the new regime of King Stork —why, exiled students from the University of Havana, many of them Fidelistas once, may attest to that.

Why bored? Why, on the typical campus nowadays, the majority of student's don't know why they have enrolled, and probably never should have enrolled at all. Back in 1962, Mr. Christopher Jenks— who later investigated, for the regents of the University of California, the background of the first Berkeley riots—published in *Harper's* an article entitled "The Next Thirty Years in the Colleges," in which he said what he could in defense of the higher learning in this land. He then estimated that on the typical campus, 1 per cent of the students desire a serious scholarly or scientific training; 2 per cent seek a more general intellectual education; perhaps 5 per cent want an introduction to upper-middle-brow culture and upper-middle-class conviviality; 20 per cent are after technical training; another 20 per cent desire merely certification as ambitious and respectable potential employees. That leaves more than half of the students; and, as Mr. Jenks put it, the majority don't know what they desire from college, and never take degrees. What with the added inducement of postponing or escaping military service, and increased recruiting by universities and colleges, matters are somewhat worse now, eight years later.

Bored students, quite aimless in the university, will embrace any university rag for diversion from the dreary routine of classes; and no inconsiderable part of the "revolutionary" students are merely idle young people, looking for a moment's excitement not to be obtained from folios. But also a good many of the more genuine students—those in Mr. Jenks' uppermost 8 per cent, say—are no less bored than are the fun-and-games undergraduates, and considerably more indignant.

"Irrelevance" is their battlecry; and there is some substance in their protest, even though most of them possess only a dim notion of what really is relevant to the higher learning. I cannot digress here concerning Relevance; I remark merely that the grievances of these better students are concerned with the curriculum and the administration of the university itself, really, though their dissent may take the form of a general denunciation of modern society. Although I am not unresponsive even to this latter distaste for the dominations and powers, the fads and foibles, of the moment, I venture to observe that the assault by students upon American institutions scarcely is so *relevant* as is the uprising of Czech or Yugoslav students against the grim regimes by which they are ruled.

Now add to this mood the personal grievance of most undergraduates and graduate students against military conscription; add to it the burning discontent of the proletariat of Academe—that is, the overworked and underpaid graduate assistants and teaching fellows. Add to it the resentment and bewilderment of Black Power students, impelled to "do their thing"—even though, as Tocqueville said of the French Revolution, "halfway down the stairs we threw ourselves out of the window to reach the ground more quickly." With these conditions in mind, one does not wonder that an impulse to pull down is at work upon the typical campus.

People with real grievances, but ignorant of political theory and institutions, are the natural prey of the ideologue. The terrible simplifiers appear, and an energumen with a tawdry set of yesteryear's anarchist or Marxist slogans can find some following on any campus. Those slogans are even less relevant to the present difficulties of the American university, or of American society, than are the dreary courses of study to which the radical students so vehemently object; but any ideology will serve as an apology and a focus for an academic mob. Parallels with Nazi and fascist and communist student movements, more than a generation ago, are ignored by the more violent student activists, sure of their own virtue and vision.

Consider an eminent ideologue of New Leftism on the campus —Mr. Tom Hayden, with whom I have debated. Hayden, principal founder of Students for a Democratic Society, yearns to ride the whirlwind and direct the storm; for painstaking reform, he has only contempt; practical remedies he disdains. His rhetoric—and his program, so far as he possesses one—are those of Jack London's pseudo-proletarian romance *The Iron Heel*. He would organize the poor and the uprooted, whom he would have rise in righteous wrath to turn the rascals out, forever. What happens when the revolution is consummated, Hayden does not inform us. Actually, when any old order has fallen, persons like Hayden—rebels by nature against any regime, craggy and impractical—promptly are disposed of by persons like Stalin and Mao and Castro. (The anarchists of Cuba are dead or imprisoned.)

When first I shared a platform with Tom Hayden, that evangel of Pull Down was organizing the poor of Newark. We spoke from a platform at the University of Michigan; and I happened to comment upon the causes and conditions of social decay and poverty in Corktown, the old Irish district of Detroit. Now Tom Hayden had been editor of the *Michigan Daily*, the student newspaper of the University of Michigan, and had held in Michigan the first convention of Students for a Democratic Society. Yet Hayden then confessed that he never had heard of Corktown, though for years he had lived about twenty-five miles distant from that slum.

It is so dull to brighten the corner where you are; so pleasant, initially, to carry a secular gospel to the gentiles of Newark, say. But presently Newark is aflame; alarmed, one seeks less perilous centers for the revolution—the ivied halls of Columbia University, say; or one flies to Hanoi, to Dar-es-Salaam, anywhere the funds of the movement will carry one for a well-publicized conference or interview. One impedes political conventions in Chicago; one taunts police; one mocks at everybody in either regular political party; one utters obscenities, complacently, at a Congressional hearing. What a charming vision of the future, chums—a revolution led by the sullen perpetual adolescent, unable to govern, unable even to dream any dreams except Londonian nightmares of violence! While the novelty endures, before the inevitable public reaction sets in, such a career is not at all unpleasant for those who like that sort of thing, it being the sort of thing they like. But as a means to the reform of the university, or to the reform of the civil social order —why, one need not labor this point.

Some time ago I saw a painting, rather in the manner of Daumier, by Renee Radell. It is called "Doing Their Thing." In the foreground stand two young men bearing placards, barring the way. On the placards is no inscription at all. The young men are grinning; and their mirth is the laughter of hyenas, for they are smug and well-fed and well-dressed nihilists. They bar the way to everything traditional and everything decent.

Renee Radell had caught perfectly the tone and temper of certain youthful anarchists, protesting against the affluent society that produced them. Their schooling, one gathers, has been costly and bad; their suburban environment has kept them from real knowledge of the world. Such sneering "revolutionaries" merely play a disagreeable game when they do their thing, and from them cannot conceivably come the intellectual and moral regeneration of the university, let alone the revitalizing of the civil social order. They are merely one side of the academic coin which bears the visage of John Hannah, say, on its other face.

There exists a moral order, says Edmund Burke, to which we are bound, willing or not—the "contract of eternal society" joining the dead, the living, and those yet unborn. There exist certain conventions and institutions that we must accept, if the civil social order is not to dissolve into the dust and powder of individuality, where every man's hand would be against every other man's. For very survival, in any society, in any age, we must submit to the traditions of civility, if you will.

But if that which is only submission to necessity should be made the object of choice, the law is broken; nature is disobeyed; and the rebellious are outlawed, cast forth, and exiled, from this world of reason, and order, and peace, and virtue, and fruitful penitence, into the antagonist world of madness, discord, vice, confusion, and unavailing sorrow.[2]

Into that antagonist world, the terrible simplifiers, the frantic ideologues, would cast us; and by revolution, they would make reform impossible. Stir the molten bronze in the cauldron, with Danton, and presently you slip, and are consumed in one agonizing moment.

Yet even if one cannot resist the temptation to stir the cauldron —even if the young revolutionary cries that one crowded hour of glorious life is worth an age without a name—still the university is a curious place to play at being a revolutionary. The perennial university student, the swaggering university instructor who cries havoc from the sanctuary of the Ivory Tower, the intemperate professor who hankers after power rather than freedom—these are shabby and self-regarding revolutionaries, deserving of Joan Baez's scorn. "He that lives in a college," wrote the young Burke, "after his mind is sufficiently stocked with learning, is like a man, who having built and rigged and victualled a ship, should lock her up in a dry dock." Those who mean to direct the world must enter the world.

We are incessantly assured by our comforters that the great bulk of American students do not participate, even on the most radical of campuses, in massive demonstration or radical organizations—and doubtless this is true. But apathy and indifference are no reasons for a society to congratulate itself. The passive average student does not assault his university; yet neither does he defend it against the revolutionary zealots. Time was when every university served as a locus of affections, and then—not long ago, either—the typical student would have dealt summarily with any Comus' rout of eccentrics—many of them "street people" not members at all of the academic community—that might have ventured to invade the quadrangle and interrupt—perhaps by arson—the university's ways. Today, on many a campus, the average student shrugs and watches

[2] Edmund Burke, *Reflections on the French Revolution* (London: E. P. Dutton & Co., Inc., 1910), p. 94—Eds.

indifferently: pull devil, pull baker. Clearly, an institution that can command no more loyalty than this is far gone in decadence. It remains little more than a dull apparatus for conferring meaningless certificates upon the lonely and faceless crowd of pseudo-scholars. When loyalty has trickled away, when the concept of a community of scholars is forgotten, the energumen and the fantastic may play what games they will.

Ideologues' pranks may injure a university irreparably, though they cannot improve it. In Egypt, in India, in much of Latin America, the universities have been unable to recover from the damage inflicted by student fanatics, whose concept of "student rights" is chiefly the right to be idle. Stifling free discussion, intimidating all opposition, abolishing standards of scholarship, the triumphant radical students in those lands have put an end to academic freedom and to academic attainment. In postwar Japan, the student political factions have so blighted scholarship that any intelligent young Japanese really desiring to learn something of his own culture must enroll at the University of Chicago's Oriental Institute, or at the Oriental schools of Harvard or Princeton or some other still-reputable American university. The logical culmination of such "progress" occurred a few years ago in Burma, when the army used heavy artillery against the University of Rangoon, leveling the campus to the ground that it might no longer shelter the communist apparatus.

"Revolution" within the universities of Egypt, India, Latin America, Japan, and Burma has not overthrown the governments of those countries; it has only overthrown right reason and moral imagination within the universities; it has only given the death blow to the academic community; it has only invited retaliation by the state; it has only injured those real students who know that the university is a place for reflection and preparation, not for theatrical violence. The results of play-revolution within American universities—even were the zealous minority of radicals to prevail on many a campus—would be no less disastrous for the intellect, and no more aggreeable to the rebels.

For the American civil social order, with all its faults, is broad at its base, prosperous, and still strongly supported by the overwhelming majority of its citizens. It cannot be overthrown by any cabal of radical utopians. If sufficiently irritated, the American public is quite capable of taking steps to terminate indefinitely the play-acting of campus radicals. And such steps might postpone for a great while, or prevent permanently, those reforms of the American college and university so urgently needed.

In a democratic age, dissidents must endeavor to win public opinion to their side; if they cannot persuade—if they alienate public opinion by their extreme measures—they must be crushed by general disapproval. In any society, organized protest must employ one of two methods. On the one hand, the dissenters may demonstrate and petition with the object of informing those in power (or the responsible public) that injustice or bad policy exists—thus, in effect, pleading visibly for a redress of practical grievances. Or on the other hand, the dissidents may endeavor to mount a massive revolt—beginning with civil disobedience, perhaps, but soon growing uncivil—meant to overthrow the existing powers; this method presupposes that the great mass of the public dimly sympathizes with the dissidents, or at least will remain inactive.

The latter undertaking would be absurd, in America today; 5 or 10 per cent of a student body cannot permanently capture a university (though they may disrupt it for some time), let alone capture the American nation. There remains the first approach, that of calling attention, through peaceable means, to justified discontents. But for a petition of grievances to be heeded, the petitioners must be sensible in their requests and decent in their methods. In that, most of the student radicals have failed. Most of all, they have failed in shallow talk of "revolution," when what they really require—and all they can possibly get, with luck—is prudent reform.

"The Sensual and the Dark rebel in vain," Coleridge wrote, "slaves by their own compulsion." The neglect of right reason and moral imagination on the typical campus may account for the unreasoning and violent character of much student protest; but also that decay makes it impossible for students themselves to plan a real improvement of the Academy—until they first emancipate themselves from the oppression of the sensual and the dark. "In God's name," said Demosthenes to the Athenians, "I beg of you to *think*." Strange though it may seem, the American university is supposed to be a center for thought. Thought lacking, among administrators, professors, and students, there remain only two possibilities: the dreary domination of people like John Hannah, or the destructive antics of people like Carl Oglesby. Neither can succeed in restoring academic community and academic vigor—for, as Talleyrand put it, you can do everything with bayonets except sit upon them.

In American society at large, it is the uprooted and dispossessed who turn to violence: as Governor George Romney pointed out (somewhat tardily), the primary cause of the Detroit riots was the Federal bulldozer—the dislodging of hundreds of thousands of people by an urban "renewal" which created urban desolation. Those dispossessed cannot work an urban revolution, let alone a national revolution; yet they can make a city dangerous and miserable. True community shattered, men cannot live in security and peace.

So it is with the academic community. Revolution cannot mend it; only patient labor and the employment of imagination can restore its loyalties. Frivolous "revolutionary" gestures by students will have no other effect than diminishing the serious voice in a university's affairs that responsible students ought to have. At Indiana University, very recently, a mock election was held to nominate a chancellor for the Bloomington campus. (Actually, the post is appointive, being under the jurisdiction of the Regents, of course; but this election was to be an expression of students' concern.) And what candidates were nominated? Why, Paul Boutelle of the Socialist Workers Party, Staughton Lynd the militant pacifist, and William Dennis the Black Power revolutionary. (One conservative student placed his own name in nomination, justly feeling himself no less qualified than these gentlemen.) What sensible undergraduate reformers!

I do not mean to express contempt for all the suggestions of the New Left people, where university reform is concerned. Some of them recommend, for instance, that the alumni be given a much larger power in the university's affairs; and I agree that it would be well to interest the alumni in something besides season tickets for the football games. But this scarcely is "revolution": indeed, it is one of the most conservative features of the old British universities, where much authority reposes in the "university court," or similar body, in which all alumni may vote annually, if they bother to attend. I am surprised that the New Left folk do not seem to have thought of proposing for American universities a kind of students' tribune, after the fashion of the rector (elected by the students, as representative of their interests) at each of the Scottish universities. (At three of the four ancient Scottish universities, I confess, the students usually choose some mountebank or passing —and absentee—celebrity as rector; but at least they have the chance to be heard in the university's deliberations.)

The revolutions of our time have not brought liberty and peace: from Moscow to Peiping, from Accra to Jakarta, they have conferred power upon squalid oligarchs—to be overthrown in turn, perhaps, by military juntas. Revolution has not brought security to Nigeria, nor fraternity to Colombia. At best, revolutions have brought such a hard master as would be anathema to intransigent professors and students. Revolution in America (*per imposible*), within the university or without it, would hideously disillusion the very utopians who talk sanguinely and sanguinarily of such possibilities.

To recognize at last that something is amiss with the higher learning in America, and with American society, is some considerable gain—worth, perhaps, the price we have paid for this knowledge through disruption. This tardy awareness may impel us to humanize the university again. Yet the university is not the Bastille, to be taken by frantic storm and razed to the ground; nor ought we to massacre the Invalides, dull dogs though some professors may be. The university is not a prison or a fortress, but a community of scholars—and not a community of one generation only. If you would reform it, understand its past greatness and its surviving promise—and, to quote Joan Baez one last time (her words in the first turbulence at Berkeley), "Do it with love."

FREEDOM IN EDUCATION: THE INTERNAL AND THE EXTERNAL CRISIS

Robert Theobald

In 1967, I tried to set out my thinking on the issue of education in a paper entitled "Education for a New Time." [1] After stating that we had to discover an educational system in which the student could fully participate, I closed with a statement of urgency:

> The time for change is now, because the potentials are here and the dangers are here. If individuals and groups do not move, do not use their resources, we soon may not be able to move! This society can close down, can become unchangeable, and can become—to put it bluntly—*evil*. The choice is ours.

Any relevant examination of the situation today must start from a clear perception of the fact that the evolution feared in this speech has become reality in large part and that the clearly foreseeable course of events shows that things must be expected to worsen further before we can hope for improvement. It is only necessary to look at the various polls to see how public sympathy is moving away from those who perceive the necessity for massive change and toward those who wish to restore law and order based on norms which have been made irrelevant by the massive technological revolution which man has himself created.[2]

During the early 1960s, the issue confronting the society was generally defined in terms of discovering how it would be possible for those who were excluded from the benefits accorded to the major-

---

[1] Published in *United Church Journal*, Vol. 5. No. 6 (March 1967), pp. 3–8.
[2] For a wider discussion of this subject see Robert Theobald, *An Alternative Future for America* (Chicago: Swallow Press, 1969).

ity of the society to participate fully. However, as we studied and
acted on this issue we discovered that it is impossible to provide
full participation for all without fundamental structural change in
the society. Today, therefore, we are confronted with a growing
demand from the various powerless groups—racial minorities, the
poor, the young, the aged, and women—that society should be so
reorganized that they are not prevented from controlling the conditions of their own lives.

This evolution of the key domestic issue is leading to a fundamental change in patterns of alliances. The "liberal" no longer per-
ceives the justice of the demands being made: he believes that there
are adequate channels of communication available in the current
society and that the structure is sound. He is therefore outraged at
the fact that groups have felt it increasingly necessary to move outside accepted channels to dramatize their cause. While he was prepared to accept that blacks had legitimate grievances leading to
volatility and anger, he finds the "uptightness" of the student without real basis and applauds measures to control it. The statement
made by Father Hesburgh at Notre Dame and the general reaction
to it clearly dramatize this reality. The new alliance only now beginning to develop is among all those who perceive the need for structural change—even though they may disagree about the nature of
the structural change which is required. This alliance sees itself confronted by structures which are designed to prevent meaningful
change in the society. It argues that this is inevitable because bureaucracies were designed to eliminate the "human element" in
decision-making. People are no longer seen as the enemy: rather
this new alliance sees the "roles" in which people are trapped as the
problems and it works to free individuals, enabling them to act in
new ways which seem more valuable to them.

For this new alliance the present crisis is a fact of life—recognized
but essentially taken for granted. Instead of trying to hold back the
incoming tide of repression like King Canute, they are determined
to ensure that the new institutions which they are creating are built
on rock and not sand. They are concerned, therefore, to create viable
models of life-styles for the future world which we are now able
to enter, in the hope that as these styles become visible they will

change the tide of public opinion. (If one wishes to preserve the analogy of King Canute and the tide, they are interested not in preventing the tide from coming in but in changing the position of the moon so that the tide of repression will recede.)

In order to produce viable new models of education and in order to influence public opinion it will be necessary to understand appropriate complete educational theory for a world of permanent change. We must learn how to teach people to make decisions for themselves rather than on the basis of structural authority.

In order to clarify the issues involved I would like to offer a new definition of the meaning of education: *Education is the process of providing each individual with the capacity to develop his potential to the full. This requires that we enlarge the individual's perceptive ability by providing a sufficiently wide range of societal environments that the talents of all can be used.*

This definition can perhaps be best enlarged upon by once again discussing the difference between education and training, a difference which has been so muddled as to have become meaningless. Education should be seen as the process of providing the individual with the skills to participate in the ongoing development of the activity with which he is concerned: in other words, he does not need to apply a rote set of rules but rather understands the principles underlying his activity. Training, on the other hand, provides a set of hard and fast rules which can be applied to a given range of situations but which do not permit further development of skills. An individual who is "educated" in an area is therefore able to adapt to change: an individual who is trained will find his knowledge becoming obsolete with change.

There is a peculiar, and far from obvious, consequence of this definition. Whether an individual is engaged in education or training does not depend on any objective set of criteria but on the individual's purpose in trying another particular area of knowledge. For example, let us look at the possible relationships between foreign languages and the knowledge of the automobile. An automobile engineer wishes to be *educated* in the automobile for his future growth depends on a sufficiently complete understanding of the automobile to be able to participate in its further development; he will therefore learn foreign languages as a skill which enables him to learn more about his chosen subject of concern: the automobile. On the other hand, the student of romance languages will wish to be *educated* in foreign languages and to be *trained* in the use of the automobile.

Refusal to accept that the value of education depends on one's purpose is snobbery: a feeling that there is a hierarchy of values in activity patterns. In other words, it is based on the belief that an "academic" is definitely and inherently more valuable than an automobile engineer or a gardener. If we are to be able to create an educational system valid for the future we must accept that the area seen as education *by the individual* will depend on his own purpose.

This implies, in turn, that there must be many styles of educational institutes for the many educations which exist already and the even wider range which will come into existence as we encourage the diversity which has been made possible by the new technologies.

The problem which confronts us at this point, however, is the process by which education, in the definition given above, can be achieved. We are increasingly aware of the routes which can be used to train people in skills. Programmed teaching machines— to an even greater extent programmed computers—will provide the best possible individualized instruction for each person. The necessary information can so be structured that each individual can proceed at his own pace and follow his own perception of his own needs.

We know very little about the ways in which "education" in the full sense given above can become reality. The remainder of this paper will therefore concentrate upon the justification for fundamental changes in the educational system and some of the initial steps which could be taken to achieve movement toward an educational system.

We can get an initial sense of the areas of concern by examining the feeling on campuses across the country that the main problem that exists is that students are cut off from both relevance and involvement. The meaning of these complaints becomes clear in the light of the discussion above, for the student is quite simply stating that his education is not being structured around his own educational purposes but rather about a structured curriculum which serves the needs of the departments, disciplines, and administrations.

This concern can be made more concrete as we examine the two basic realities of patterns of knowledge. First, they are static and not dynamic. The disciplines in which most students work are without a sense of the continuing evolution of the issues in the theoretical and the real worlds. Textbooks and teachers are more concerned with teaching the present set of conclusions derived from the present set of assumptions than with giving the student a sense of the ways in which both assumptions and conclusions have changed over time, let alone with giving the student a set of tools for participating in the further evolution of the subject. To put it bluntly, most teachers are insufficiently sure of their own competence to welcome their students as joint creators of knowledge, and therefore do not provide them with the tools to surpass them. The good teacher, on the other hand, knows no greater moment than when a former student reaches the point where he can teach the former teacher.

Second, the styles of academic learning and teaching are so structured that they exclude the relevance of emotion. It is assumed that the introduction of emotion will inevitably destroy the validity of the work. It is not yet realized that there is a critical and rather simple distinction which can and must be drawn. Goals and purposes are not objective—they depend upon subjective reasoning about what is important to the individual and the group.[3] Once groups have been set, then it is possible to analyze objectively what should be done to reach goals. The decision to preserve the objective analytical style of the university therefore means that the individual can only be involved in the "how" and not the "why."

There are many who would argue that the university should only be concerned with "how"—that it is not a place for the discovery of

[3] At a higher level of analysis, based on cybernetic and general system analysis, it is possible to argue that there is no valid distinction between subjective and objective analysis. The terms used in the body of the piece accord, however, with current perceptions of reality.

partisan views but for the analysis of alternative possibilities. There are two problems with such an approach. The first and the most obvious is that there will always be an overwhelming tendency to analyze how to achieve the goals which already exist. The analysis of the rote to these goals increases the likelihood that the analyzed steps will in fact take place and therefore lead to the goals which are presently accepted whether they are valid or not. It is insufficiently recognized that "self-fulfilling" prophecy is one of the most fundamental of all realities: one achieves what one desires. Thus, analyses of what "might be" tend to create the possibilities which are discussed. (It should be obvious that if the society has no opposing goals except those currently accepted it becomes impossible to expect any change in the society. Thus the decision of the university to cut itself off from subjective analysis deprives the society of one of the possible areas in which new goal-creation can occur.)

In addition, and even more critically, it is now clear that the brain is organized along subjective rather than objective lines. One's thought patterns are created in terms of satisfying one's own needs and conditioned responses are created according to past experiences which satisfied one's personal needs. Changes in such thought patterns will only occur if the individual is brought to perceive subjectively—that his present thought patterns do not maximize his satisfaction.

In other words it is a tautology that "each individual will always act in such a way as to maximize his satisfaction at the moment he makes a decision given all the circumstances of which he is aware." This statement has, of course, no content for it applies to both the individual who knocks a woman down to steal her purse and the person who risks his life to save that of another. Change occurs when people alter their views about the actions which seem to them to be "most satisfactory" and this is only possible—by definition—when their subjective views are changed.

These points can be made clearer by an examination of theories developed by Gregory Bateson, a psychologist and anthropologist now working in Hawaii. The description given below has been heavily adapted from his original work but remains true, I believe,

to his purposes.[4] He has shown that there are various levels of learning and that each level of learning is associated with certain structural requirements. The first level of learning is the simple perception of a fact—for example, an individual enters a room. The second
level of learning occurs when the two facts are interrelated—
"When the bell rings I go to lunch." The third level of learning occurs when an individual improves his performance within an existing system of understanding—"If I go to lunch an hour before the
bell rings, I have to stand in line but I will get food. If I go to lunch
an hour after the bell rings, I will get my food immediately but it
will be leftovers." The fourth level of learning occurs when one is
able to perceive the nature of the present systems and to re-examine
them with a view to discovering how the total system can be
changed. If we stay in the area of food as an example, we might
wish to re-examine the nature of the human body to discover what
real options there are to present inherited patterns of eating habits
given the fact that we now need far fewer calories both because we
are kept artificially warm and because we need to carry out far less
physical effort.

To what do these levels of learning correspond in real life? The
first level occurs when the child reaches the stage when he can distinguish among stimuli rather than perceiving all life as a single
Gestalt. The second stage occurs when two realities are intercon-
nected for the first time: for example, the young duckling discovers
his mother and is then programmed by instinct to follow her—
it has been shown that the "mother" can be a wide range of objects
rather than the actual mother. (In this connection, it is clear that
the Pavlovian experiments are simply a special case of level 2 learning—that it is possible to relate any two experiences together if
they are reinforced a sufficient number of times.)

The third level of learning is the one which our present systems
of "education" are geared to achieve—they are designed to make it
possible to improve our level of performance within our present perceptions of the state of the universe. In the new terminology used

---

[4] Bateson's original terminology, which is highly technical, would be con-
fusing to the nonexpert: for example he talks about zero levels of learning.

above, the entire "educational" system is concerned with training and not education. The effect of this pattern is that people are taught about realities. The revolt against the school and university system comes from a spreading realization that the present understanding of the social system is invalid. This is particularly obvious for the ghetto school where the real world is teacher rather than those human beings playing the role of teacher; but we are rapidly coming to realize that the problem is not confined to the ghetto.[5]

We are therefore beginning to see the need for fourth-level learning: i.e., learning which permits us to change our perceptions of the world we live in. But we have not yet realized that the styles which make possible fourth-level learning are contradictory to those needed in third-level situations. In other words, the methods used for training are profoundly unsuitable for real education. Given this reality, we must take seriously the particularly permanent character of our thinking because of the very nature of brain structuring and also because of the fact that all societies are so structured as to prevent fourth-level learning.

This is the meaning of Arnold Toynbee's statement that cultures have not, in the past, adapted to fundamental changes in their environment. In effect, he is arguing that these cultures have never been able to achieve the fourth-level thinking necessary to change their basic understandings of the world and to develop new structures and institutions appropriate to the new world which the society had entered. We are now going through our own "Toynbee crisis" and whether or not we can deal with it will depend on our ability to create the conditions for fourth-level learning.

Fourth-level learning requires that people move outside their present perceptions of reality, see reality in a new way, and thus discover and accept new patterns of behavior. Three overall routes to fourth-level learning appear to be emerging.

First, there is the wide range of processes being developed to help individuals, either singly or in small groups, to break out of their current Skinner boxes.[6] The aim is to develop new patterns of

[5] For a particularly sensitive understanding of this issue see the piece by Robert Coles in the Fall 1968 issue of *Daedalus*.

[6] A Skinner box is a closed space in which animals are confronted with a

goals which would enable people to begin the process of overcoming their weaknesses and thus develop their own human potential. The theory behind this approach is that it is more valuable to develop one's potential strengths than to concentrate on eliminating one's weaknesses. The Human Potential Seminar is one of the best known of these techniques—it operates by freeing people to set immediately achievable personal goals and by developing the scope of these goals over the period of the seminar.[7]

The second route is to develop a social situation in which people can join together around a common goal which is more important to those involved than the ideologies by which they presently live. It has been proved on innumerable occasions that the search for an effective strategy will cause people to develop and accept new models which will challenge their existing conditioned responses. However, it is increasingly clear that involvement in an experience of the first type listed above may be necessary before many human beings are ready for involvement in the development of a social purpose.

The third route is to introduce a wide range of new ideas which effectively challenge all existing idea patterns. This can be done, for example, by an imaginative speaker who attacks the "sacred cows" of all ideologies rather than a single one and in so doing provides new sets of ideas to various people in the audience. It can also be done using the modern media—radio, film, TV—where the content of the media production creates a new Gestalt which encourages change in personal thinking. It can also be done by several people who hold different views dialoguing together rather than engaging in sterile debate among fixed opinions. In all these cases, however, it appears essential that those individuals who hear or see these presentations must have an opportunity to be involved in

---

choice of positive and negative sanctions—or to use more colloquial terms, the whip and the carrot. It can be proved that so long as the space is closed and there are no other options, the only "intelligent" form of behavior is to accept the pleasant and to avoid the unpleasant. This reality changes so soon as it is possible to structure realities: people can then create new experiences for themselves.

[7] Information about Human Potential Seminars can be obtained by writing to Stone-Brandel Center, 1439 S. Michigan, Chicago, Illinois.

their discussion in a significant way, or the new input will not "stick." [8]

The first profound difference in fourth-level learning is that the methods of measuring success change as we alter levels. It is impossible to spell out all the differences here but it is essential to mention some of them briefly. Success in third-level learning is measured by objective tests such as grades; fourth-level learning can only be measured by subjective criteria.

The second profound difference is in one's attitude toward those unlike oneself and who do not share one's knowledge and beliefs. In objective learning it is rather generally felt that there are certain things that everyone should know and that it is therefore justified to force people to participate in certain courses—thus the requirements for certain core curricula, etc. In fourth-level learning, on the other hand, one realizes that each person has different areas in which he wishes to be educated and that it is both useless and immoral to force the individual to be involved in courses which do not interest him.

In other words, one can only affect individuals who share real interests. Rather, therefore, than trying to involve everybody with one's concerns, one should be content to work with core groups who already share common interests. If the concerns are real and important, their development over time by the core group will lead others to become interested.

In particular we must understand that we cannot change a person's ideas by attacking his presently held beliefs: we can be effective if we add new conditioned responses to those he already holds. This means that one must involve any individual starting from the point at which he now is rather than forcing him to share one's own set of concerns. In order to do this one must be prepared to accept that he may be wrong and the other person may be right: in other words, one must be ready to work within *his* reality if one is to have any hope of changing him.

It is for this reason that attempts at human contact between peo-

[8] An extensive report on this subject entitled *Communication to Build the Future Environment* can be obtained by writing to Don Imsland, Human Design, 212 West Franklin, Minneapolis, Minnesota 55404.

ple who are intensely antagonistic have no chance of success. A black separatist and a white racist—to use two common labels— fear entering each others' reality and therefore simply attack the surface symbols of the other party. The necessary attempt to discover new realities so as to engage in fourth-level learning can only start by talking to people whose ideas are sufficiently similar to one's own that they are not too threatening, so that one is not afraid to try to understand fully the reality from which the other individual operates.

It is at this point that the profound clash between existing third-level (training) institutions and future fourth-level (educational) institutions becomes most acute. The process of sharing ideas cannot be limited by structural authority—i.e., authority derived from one's position. If fourth-level education is to occur one must only accept sapiential authority—i.e., authority resulting from the knowledge of the particular field under discussion and the acceptance of this knowledge by the others involved.[9]

It is still insufficiently understood that the tension of today does not derive from differential sapiential authority but rather from the fact that too many of those with structural authority do not possess the sapiential authority to make their decisions intelligent. It is clear, at least to me, that students have been—and still are—asking faculty and administration to join with them in creating new structures in which sapiential authority is the source of the necessary decision-making.

I am not implying—nor I believe are the vast majority of students —that students hold all the sapiential authority or indeed most of it. They are only asking for recognition of the fact that in today's world, where many of the young have sapiential authority simply by the fact that they are nearer to the new conditions than we are, they should be allowed to participate fully insofar as they are competent. We should take seriously the statement by Margaret Mead that today all those who are over thirty are pilgrims in a shaky land.

In addition, I am not suggesting that we should fall into the trap

[9] These terms were developed by T. T. Patterson.

of assuming that all we have to do is to inform students that we recognize that they have sapiential authority and that they should go ahead and exercise it. This is the statement which has been used by many of the experimental colleges and it effectively guts the student by providing him with far more freedom than he can effectively handle. Our responsibility is to provide conditions in which the individual can come to perceive his own sapiential authority and learn to contribute where it is most relevant. I am convinced that it is equally immoral to assume sapiential authority before it really exists as it is to deny the possibility of its creation.

In all our relations with human beings we have the responsibility to help them to structure for themselves situations within which they grow; a useful rule of thumb might well be "what one already handles plus 10 per cent for risk." It seems to me that this rule is as relevant for the very young child as for the full-grown adult: the recognition of the potential for failure if one oversteps one's capacities is as critical for a healthy human being as the recognition of one's enormous potential power to do what one desires.

The creation of the possibility for fourth-level learning on the campuses across the country requires as many different techniques as there are campuses. Change in specific situations depends upon the "political" realities of each campus. There are, however, some patterns which may have some general validity and they are listed below. It is critical, however, to realize that these ideas can only be valuable if they are completely subordinated to a full understanding of the nature of the campus under consideration. There are no "cookbook" recipes for campus change.

1. *Creation of problem-centered courses which combine the study of the problem with action to deal with it.* Care should be taken to study problems which are within the competence of the student lest they worsen the problem under consideration. Few materials have yet been produced to support such problem-centered courses; one initiative is the Dialogue Series of books.[10]

[10] The books in the Dialogue series are designed to make it possible for students to discover the present state of knowledge in a particular subject. Titles now available are *Dialogue on Poverty, Dialogue on Technology, Dialogue on Education, Dialogue on Science, Dialogue on Youth, Dialogue on*

2. *Elimination of the grading system over time.* There are many ways of chipping away at the system—pass–fail, pass–no-fail, subjective grading, class grading. It is probably relatively unimportant which route one uses as long as it is realized that the ultimate objective is to get to the point where the critical indicator is the subjective view of the person about the value of the course he took.

3. *Courses which do not last a full semester*—or which spill over into a new semester, or last until the instructor determines that all the possible learning has taken place, etc.; in other words, any set of techniques which can begin to eliminate the assumption that knowledge is necessarily fashioned in four-month hunks.

4. *Creation of a "neutral point"*—in which all those concerned with the future of the campus can meet together on an extended basis to discover what should be done in a setting which bars challenge to motivation and assumes commitment to change.

5. *A change in the nature of the student body*—so that the divisions between faculty and student become less obvious: bringing in middle-aged and experienced individuals, who have different visions of the society, etc.

6. *Involving the university in the community*—so that it becomes possible to eliminate the concept that one is being educated *or* one is living. It seems clear that one of the necessary changes of the next generations is that we cease to see life as being for earning and begin to see life as being for learning.[11]

7. *On a far more general level, the creation of an information system*—which will inevitably require computers by which the student can gain information about what he needs to know immediately—is, I would argue, the necessary base for most of the foregoing changes. As I see it, he should be able to find out about the present state of knowledge in each problem/possibility area, the range of activities now occurring on campus, and the interests of

---

Women, and *Dialogue on Violence.* In preparation are *Dialogue on Dialogue, Dialogue on Urban Living, Dialogue on Health,* and *Dialogue on Black Power.* All books are available from Bobbs Merrill in Indianapolis at $1.25.

[11] I owe this formulation to Don Benson.

others on the campus so that he can find the like-minded people with whom he could work successfully. The threat of big brother would be avoided by each person having the right to determine what he wanted to have put on the computer.

Any or all of these steps may be relevant on a particular campus, but I still remain convinced that the most appropriate first step on many campuses is to change the nature of the incoming class. There are two important reasons for this approach. First, there is no doubt that each incoming freshman class is better informed and more "turned-on" that the one that preceded it. Second, freshmen come up believing that the campus is as the catalogue says that it is— if they are reinforced in this belief their actions may succeed in creating the type of campus which is required and already described in the catalogue. In addition, we should always remember that freshmen have four years to affect the campus.

There are two significant possible patterns of action. First, one might create a new style of freshman orientation designed to discover which of the incoming students are already excited about an area and to place them in touch with faculty who have the skills to help them to develop. The process might start with the mailing of a book to all incoming students—possible choices would include *How Children Learn* by John Holt, *Compulsory Miseducation* by Paul Goodman, or my own *An Alternative Future for America*. Many other books would be suitable—the only requirement being that they invite thought rather than putting across completed concepts.

When the freshmen arrived on campus one of the parts of freshman orientation would be a continuous film show designed to "blow their minds" or, more technically, randomize their synapses. The exit from the cinema would be through a room where there would be a continuous bull session so that those who wanted to talk would have an opportunity to do so. Those who were really interested would then be offered two opportunities. First, they would be asked what they would like to learn. If this were not possible within the current university setup, courses would then be created grouping those students with similar interests. We now have sufficient experience with creating free universities so that the mechanics of this process should not be difficult.

Second, there would be tables in an adjoining room where those who needed advice on which major they should take, or which courses they should take within their major, would be able to ask students and faculty members from each major field. The object would be to help students to find those courses and those professors who could be most likely to provide them with the sort of education which they thought relevant.

The basic requirement for such a freshman orientation program is that a significant number of those in senior classes be prepared to stop taking out their frustrations on the incoming students and to be prepared to work honestly with them. There is also a need for a significant number of faculty to be involved if the turned-on student is not to find himself in a turned-off class.

Innovations in freshman orientation of this type have occurred across the country already; and there has usually been little difficulty in making these changes, for those in charge of freshman orientation have usually been uninterested. This does not hold true for the other step, which appears essential if freshmen are to reach the point where they can participate fully in a meaningful university program. We need a freshman introductory year which will give them the necessary skills to be able to be involved in fourth-level learning.

First, we need a crash course in social reality. This would be based on feasible developments in the sciences, the technology, and the socioeconomy. Each third week, students would be provided with data about a possible development and then would be asked to brainstorm for about three weeks about the importance of the development, the way in which it could best be introduced, the dangers it might involve, etc. It would be made perfectly clear that there were no "correct" answers.

The second course would be in how to think logically. This would involve the practice of such techniques as inductive and deductive logic, etc. Great care, however, would be taken to insure that the student was not paralyzed by words; rather the individual would be placed in a situation where he would learn the techniques and only later discover that he had been engaged in "difficult" tasks.

The third course would teach the methods which can be used to create new ideas. The popular word for this is "grooving"—the process by which the knowledge possessed by the group at the end of a session is greater than that which was available to any single member at the beginning. The technical term for this is synergy— a descriptive word for the processes which occur in nature and elsewhere which lead $1+1$ to equal $3+$.

The final course would be in perception; here the freshman student would learn skills enabling him to perceive a wider range of the phenomena by which he is surrounded. At one level, this is an art course; but the object is not to help the student appreciate existing artworks, not even to help him to create art for himself— although this might be a desirable by-product—but only to learn to use his senses to widen his own perception.

We are now at the point where we shall either succeed in creating and communicating the new educational models or we can expect public pressure to become so great that "education" will become impossible. The education which I have suggested here is not designed to force change on anybody—rather it believes that our only hope is to develop ideas which are inherently so powerful that they make their own way in the world. John Maynard Keynes, the great British economist, stated that sooner or later it is ideas and not men which rule the world; our goal today must be to reduce the amount of time between the creation of an idea and its evaluation and subsequent introduction if it is proved to be valid.

If our efforts are to be fully successful we must somehow create better means of communication so that we cease to "reinvent the wheel" as each college starts to be engaged in educational reform.

THE UNIVERSITY AND THE
REVOLUTION: NEW LEFT OR
NEW RIGHT?

Edmund S. Glenn

During a period of time extending a year or two into the past, and an unknown amount into the future, and which can be roughly identified with 1968 and '69, student revolts have rocked countries as distant geographically as France or Germany and China, and as distant in political ideology and organization as Czechoslovakia or Yugoslavia and the United States. Even if, for the sake of manageability, China and the European Communist countries are left out of the analysis, these revolts amount to a major social movement, possibly comparable in scope to that of 1848—another series of widespread revolts which somehow failed to lead to any true revolution.

That is, if the student revolts of 1968 can be genuinely described as *a* social movement, then a common identity ascribed to mutually uncoordinated and often disparate events exists. It should not be overlooked that each student revolt had characteristics of its own. Each was tied to a series of grievances, more or less specific in their formulation, more or less tied to the university itself. These ranged from freedom of speech on campus to overcrowding of classrooms, from draft policies to the inapproachability of professors. Whether one considers them valid depends largely on one's personal or political orientation—yet it is likely that a reasonably unbiased person would consider some of them justified, some belonging to an arena other than the university, and some simply put on as tangible pretexts for the expression of deep but intangible discontent.

It is this discontent—exhibited in its existence but almost mysterious in its origin—which forms the common denominator across nations and continents. Speaking to students (or at least to some students) in France, Germany, and Italy is like speaking to students (some students) in the United States. Specific grievances and points of negotiation with the faculty, the administration or the Ministry are soon forgotten, the war in Vietnam simply cannot be talked about in the same manner by those who are likely to be drafted into it and by those whose own Indochina war is now a matter of history. What remains, the common denominator, is a passionate conviction of being right without much clarity as to what it is that one is right about, an often iron-willed determination to act without much by way of a specification of goals, and a deep hatred against something called the System.

Explanations of events of great scope must be sought in backgrounds of great generality. It is not the coincidence in time between the overcrowding of an amphithéatre at the Sorbonne with the absenteeism of a Columbia professor called to Washington for consultations which can explain 1968. There must be something more broadly behavioral, more generally human, which, for reasons not immediately meeting the eye, came to a paroxysm at this moment of history.

Could the reason be, as the students in revolt are prone to say, the System itself, its oppressiveness increasing straw by straw until the camel's back came to break? But which system? The capitalist system? It is, if anything, mellowing. Some (and I am one of them, as was the late Harvard economist Sumner Slichter) even say that capitalism has all but disappeared, at least from the industrialized countries.

Student graffiti on the campus at Nanterre near Paris (the place at which "modern," on-campus education was being experimented with as a reaction against the impersonality of the enormous University of Paris proper) provide a clue to an answer: the revolution, they proclaimed, must go on until the day when the last capitalist is hanged with the guts of the last bureaucrat. For "bureaucrat," in this context, read orthodox Communist bureaucrat. Could it be that the System stands, very directly, for any way of life or thought which is systematic, rule-bound, impersonal, as opposed to the spontaneous, the free, the intensely and therefore personally felt?

The opposition—and the complementarity—between the spontaneous and the systematic are so obvious that we hardly ever feel a need to think about them. Yet the relationship between the two terms deserves some thought, for itself, and also because it may bring to light some of the essential characteristics of the crisis of our time.

One point at which to begin may be a little word game. Which two of the three sentences below have approximately the same meaning? Which one is different from the other ones, odd in their company?

1. "It is beautiful weather we're having."

2. "Sunny, maximum temperature in the middle fifties, probability of precipitation near zero."

3. "Haven't we met before?"

The seeming obviousness of synonymy between sentences 1 and 2 is such that most of those asked the question suspect a trap. Couldn't the point be that 2 lacks a verb? that 3 is interrogative? In the absence of stated criteria (of a systematic approach) any grouping may be defended. But if the criterion is that of the type of social situations in which the phrases are used, and of the type of message they are intended to convey, the similarity of 1 and 2 appears a possible but improbable one. The probability is that sentence 1 is said by a person aware of the state of the weather, not in response to a question, but as an opening to another person fully as aware of it as is the speaker. And, of course, what it really means in such cases is something like "Let's be friendly, to the extent the situation calls for it"—which is also the usual intent of sentence 3.

If such is the case, there must be a deep difference in logic between the two types of usage, represented by 1 (and 3, which has at this point outlived its usefulness and will no more be referred to) on the one hand and by 2 on the other.

Suppose a visitor from Mars, from a culture with entirely different usages, comes to this country, and is supplied with an excellent English–Martian dictionary and a perfect analytic grammar of the English language. Diligent study of sentence 2, decomposed into its elements, searched for the best word equivalents in Martian, recomposed according to the rules of English syntax, may conceivably yield its meaning. Not so with sentence 1. No decomposition, search for equivalents, resynthesis, will ever yield to the translation of "Let's be friendly." It is a meaning which either is known from usage—which is spontaneously felt—or else which cannot be discovered, short of the study of the entire culture of which it is one of the customs.

Sentence 2 can be taken apart and decomposed into its elements. Keeping the form of the whole, but changing each element in a specific manner, changes the overall meaning in a way easy to understand and even to predict. "Maximum in the middle nineties" differs in a precise way from "Maximum in the middle fifties." Even situations never experienced before can be meaningfully described; we know what "maximum in the upper two-hundreds" would mean.

There is no use in varying the elements of sentence 1. "Isn't the weather lovely?" has the same meaning as the original version. In fact, 1 has no elements: it is a syntagm, a whole, it is to be understood holistically or not to be understood at all. This undivided wholeness extends even beyond the expression itself: it is the entire situation which makes it up. Sentence 1 does not mean the same "Let's be friendly" when addressed by a member of a congregation to his minister as when addressed by a young man to a pretty girl.

As for the possibility of extrapolation of 1, it is most vague where that of 2 had been precise. It is not the saying, nor even the way of saying it, nor the present situation by itself, which determines the extent of friendship proffered or accepted. In contradistinction to 2, sentence 1 can be intensely personal; its effect—its very meaning—depends on who says it to whom. The extrapolation, if any, is in the persons, not the statement.

With regard to the meaning of 2, neither the person of the speaker nor that of the listener are of any great importance. However, a lot of other things are. Is the statement true? Thermometers, barometers, wind gages, the entire stuff—the entire *system*—of meteorology becomes involved. If the originator of the sentence intervenes, it is qua meteorologist, qua social role—not qua person. In fact, it is highly unlikely that one person, even shorn of such irrelevant attributes as looks, temper, or goodness, is the originator: in all probability it is an organization, with many people fulfilling different roles within it, and with its own position in the social system defined in the impersonal terms of role and function rather than in the more personal ones of families, communities, or friendships.

Clearly, understanding the meaning of 2 depends on the understanding of a system—and the capacity of making statements like it calls for belonging to a system, for playing a role in it, for acting in accordance with the definition of the role among other equally impersonal roles making up the whole structure.

The key word of this structure is *irrelevance*.

A meteorologist reads temperatures and pressures, correlates instruments, calculates the significance of weather messages coming from places he has never visited and from people he has never seen. All this he must do well—but whether his girl loves him— or, for that matter whether he is male or female—is irrelevant.

In contradistinction to this, everything in 1 is relevant. Not only what is said, but who says it and who listens; a saying, a smile, a blush, flowers in the breeze, people drawn to one another, perhaps love. The meaning is all in the situation; all of the situation is in the meaning. "Let us be friendly to the extent the situation calls for it"—and the measure of the situation's call seems to be the spontaneities of two people meeting face-to-face.

The very fact that, when asked the meaning of sentence 1, we hesitate, are not even sure we know, and tend to confuse it with the meaning of 2—and yet that when confronted by someone saying 1 we react to it every time as to the overture it is—this very fact seems to prove the naturalness, the spontaneity, of the usage.

Yet is it really so spontaneous, so natural, so unsystematic?

To speak about the weather when meaning to break the ice is a cultural convention. The limits, inner and outer, of the friendliness called for by given situations are part of the customs of the culture. E. T. Hall has shown that even the distance at which we stand from the person we address, when uttering this platitude or anything else, is determined by the culture. And every culture is a system.

Yet the difference between the two modes persists. In the way of speaking of which 1 is an example—and in the way of living of which speaking in stereotype is an archetype—the culture system dominates, but it does so unobtrusively. Cultural conventions make up a system so deeply internalized that it has become subconscious. Not being conscious of a system so pervasive that it appears to be nature itself, we follow its dictates while feeling unfettered and free.

In contradistinction to this, the way of speaking, and the way of living, of which 2 is an example implies a system which one is still learning, of the rules of which one is unavoidably conscious.

This is the difference between the "born" fullback on the day of the game, running in a way which seems to come naturally, and the same man in training, rehearsing painfully a change in pacing which might improve his performance at some future time.

It is not against a pattern of expression that the student revolt is directed—even though it is not by pure chance that it was preceded and foreshadowed by a fashion of disrespect for disciplined and grammatical use of language. As it was mentioned above, the two styles of expression involved are indicative of two ways of thought, which find also their expressions in two ways of organizing society.

The discursive style of "maximum temperature in the lower fifties, etc." may be termed *abstractive:* from a totality which includes sun, breeze, and even one's subjective mood, it abstracts such things as temperature, barometric pressure, humidity index, and studies each of them separately, as if all the other factors (by now called variables) were irrelevant. This, indeed, is the way of the learner—and of the problem-solver: the learner, be he a football player or an army recruit, decomposes motions into components to be learned "by the numbers"; the problem-solver, at whatever level, decomposes the complexity of a situation into variables to be studied and described one-by-one.

The spontaneous style of "What a beautiful day" can be termed *associative:* to the apparent content of the expression, the weather, are associated such unmentioned but all-important elements as the attitude of the speaker toward the listener. The expression, the situation, anything else which comes to mind, are associated in an undivided whole. It is the way of the poet whose rhythms, similes, and metaphors suggest unending associations of feelings.

This much was clear when we analyzed the two expressions. Putting it explicitly may serve to introduce the two types of social organization—and even more of the bases of social trust—with which each of these manners of thinking correlate.

To trust someone it is necessary to be able to predict his actions. This is why we fear the insane, whose actions seemingly follow no pattern. This is why we often mistrust strangers whose actions follow patterns different from our own.

A society can function only on the basis of trust among its members. To venture about his business, a man must trust, at the very least, that the probability of attack against him is small, and that the community will come to his help should an attack occur. In other words, he must trust certain hypotheses he is making about the behavior of others, as they trust hypotheses they make about him: society demands mutual predictability.

Such mutual predictability can be obtained in two manners, diametrically opposed to each other:

(1) First, the human group concerned may be made up of people who have been brought up in similar or mutually complementary manners, who share habits and patterns of behavior, who react alike to the same circumstances, and predictably to one another; even who think alike—in other words who have internalized the same culture, who share the same collective subconscious. Predictability among them is "natural"; no explicitly stated rules of behavior are necessary to insure it: spontaneous similarity suffices. This is the associative way of building society. Ferdinand Tönnies coined a name for it: *Gemeinschaft,* or community.

(2) The human group concerned is made up of people who do

not know each other well enough to trust one another spontaneously. Social trust can be maintained only through a system of
explicit rules, which every member of society must learn, and
which must be enforced by an apparatus of guardians of law and
order. This is known in the jargon as *Gesellschaft,* or society.

There is little doubt in my mind which of the two basic systems
I would prefer to dream about: "spontaneity" is a much nicer
word than "enforcement." In addition, the word "apparatus" sends
cold shivers down my spine and, as the Romans used to say, who
will guard me against the guardians?

Yet there is equally little doubt as to which system I would
choose in reality—and it would not be the same one.

Small human groupings, leading relatively uncomplicated lives,
stemming from the same stocks and sharing from childhood the
same experiences, can afford to be communities. Living by shared
traditions, they do not need to learn more than they know—and
they do not need to know that all the do's and don't's which appear
to them obvious, natural, and necessary are in fact the artificial
products of one specific culture.

We—the people of the twentieth century—are not a small grouping with relatively uncomplicated lives. We stem from many
stocks, we impinge upon one another, we are barely—and much
too slowly—learning to live with one another. And as long as we
are learning, we need explicit rules, the enforcement of rules—
in fact all the irritating reminders of human unfreedom.

Let me make it clear that my thesis is not a simple appeal for
social discipline of the "law-and-order" type, with rules followed
simply because they are rules, and society defended without any
questioning of its structure and purpose. The appeal is mainly
for intellectual discipline, and the purpose the very same which
guides the self-proclaimed revolutionaries on our campuses—the
counterrevolutionaries in my language. This purpose is to insure
mutual toleration, perhaps even mutual friendship, among the
many communities which make up a society such as ours. The
purpose is—ultimately—human freedom: something impossible in
a state of affairs where groupings are at each other's throats, de-

manding unquestioned loyalty from the members of each in-group in a time of danger.

To put it somewhat more concretely:

Until I moved recently to a small university town, I used to live in the inner city of Washington. I was still living there at the time of the riots which followed the assassination of Martin Luther King, and sometime thereafter. In the days following the disturbances the situation in our neighborhoods was tense. Blacks and whites who did not know one another personally tended to view each other with suspicion.

One afternoon I went into a pastry shop. Two Negro shoppers were there at the time, obviously young gentlemen. I selected a huge cake for a family occasion; the salesgirl placed it in a box and followed with the ritual "Will that be all?" I replied that it should be enough to go with my cup of coffee. The two young men doubled up with laughter.

As an attempt at humor, my remark was extremely feeble. And I have no reason to believe that the young men's sense of humor was either so crude or so overdeveloped as to make them think otherwise. In reality both my remark and their laughter had a different meaning: my message was that we were all simply human and not antagonists; their laughter meant that they had understood and that they agreed.

This is associative usage at its best: an instantaneous unfreezing, an immediate understanding of community. But if it could work this way it is because neither the two young men nor I were racists to begin with. Had they been racists, no amount of corny jokes on my part (or even of good ones) would have made them change their mind. Had I been a racist, I would have interpreted their laughter as the confirmation of a contemptuous stereotype.

Associative usage can make us recognize common belonging; it does not create it.

If we want to see by what logic (it is more difficult in practice) prejudices are shed, in-groups are enlarged, and out-groups made to appear less threatening, it is toward the abstractive mode that we have to turn.

Let us look at the following statements: "My tooth hurt, so I went to a black dentist." "My tooth hurt, so I went to a white dentist." "My tooth hurt, so I went to an Asian dentist." "My tooth hurt, so I went to a French welder." The last one is nonsense. Obviously not because "French" has been substituted for "black," "white," or "Asian," but because "welder" substituted for "dentist" appears in the wrong context.

Even in less obvious cases, such substitutions make us notice that part of the information which is irrelevant. In the context of my earlier example, it would show that it was irrelevant that the two young men were black; what was relevant was that they were gentlemen; had I thought them ruffians—white or black—I would have acted, and felt, differently.

But the cost is there: in order to recognize the irrelevance of race or nationality or family ascendance, in order to avoid *ascribing* to others the characteristics (true or much more often supposed) of the basic human grouping from which they come, and to view them in terms of their pertinent *achievements,* one has to disregard much of what makes up their wholeness.

The same change is called for when turning from the others to oneself. To acquire—simultaneously—a knowledge of the world around us and a tolerance for others, each of us must proceed through a series of decentrations (in the words of Jean Piaget), to cease accepting things as they look from the point of one's subjective particularity, to coordinate one's ego-centered observations with those of others—in other words to abstract, and in the process to lose or at least subordinate a part of the self, to accept being learners and to postpone spontaneity.

All this may look pretty thin—"to lack relevance"—when compared to the heady slogans of "social justice," "social consciousness," "the system," or "the establishment," or other words with little by way of real referents but great aptitude at expressing the hangups of those who mouth them.

Yet it is serious and deep-reaching business, as the following example, for all its seeming triviality, may show:

Take a sentence such as "See you later." It is possible to substitute a different word or phrase for each word in it. For example

"See you at five." or "See you at home." We can obtain in this manner, in the last position, all the adverbs or adverbial phrases of the English language. As a matter of fact, the method of substitution is used by linguists to study the parts of speech of hitherto unanalyzed languages. This possibility of substitution, with corresponding changes in semantic value, marks the sentence as belonging to the abstractive mode.

"See you later" can be changed into "See you later, alligator." Now substitution is no longer possible. "See you at five, alligator" is nonsense.

But if something—abstraction—has been taken away from the sentence, something else has been added: association, in this case an expression of social solidarity. "See you later, alligator" is a pseudo-secret way of saying "See you later, buddy." One does not say that to just anyone. And the secrecy of the code, pseudo though it may be, adds to its value: a true brother knows the countersign "In a while, crocodile." This may be an old or even obsolete fad, but the very fact that it has been a fad proves that it did hit a responsive chord.

"See you later, alligator" may have eliminated the possibility of substitution, but it allowed among those who could exchange it without artificiality an immediate expression of human warmth.

Can the loss of facility for grammatical substitution matter, if what is gained is human warmth?

The fact is that it does—tragically. Basil Bernstein has shown that boys in England develop differently depending on whether the abstractive usage or the associative usage predominates in their environments. Where associative expression dominates, usually in the working class, there is a loss rather than a gain in the verbal component of the IQ during the crucial years of secondary education. The ability to strike out in a technological and systematic society is impaired, often fatally. The in-group solidarity developed through associative usage compensates for it only partially: the in-groups concerned are stuck on the lower rungs of the social ladder.

On the other hand, the only trustworthy method for bringing about permanent improvements in the IQ's of culturally deprived youngsters is a linguistic drill derived from the methods of foreign-language teaching—make all the possible substitutions: "The boy has a dog," "The boy has a cat," "The girl had a dog" . . . substitution, systematization at its purest.

There is more to this than quibbling for educationists. It is the substance of a tragic dilemma: many children—many people—cannot be reached except in the associative mode; but reaching them will do little good, unless it can bring them to acting in the abstractive mode. And the two modes are in constant opposition.

Or, to put it somewhat differently, associative usage is profoundly human, which abstractive usage is not—but it is inhumane to leave youngsters in the state of inadaptation to which the associative lack of intellectual discipline would condemn them.

But, once again, is it worth subverting spontaneity, the feeling of human belonging, for the sake of adaptation to the abstractions of a technological society?

I believe I have already answered this question. Technology—even though without it millions would starve—is not the sole or even the main product of abstractive thought. The main product is logical thought, and only logical thought can bring about mutual toleration. There is no stronger weapon against prejudice than the scientific study of its rumors and its stereotypes. And only those trained in abstractive thought are capable of deriving benefit from such studies.

I may be skating on pretty thin ice at this point, by analyzing the revolt of 1968 as a revolt against systematic thinking, an opposition between the pseudo-freedom of association and the genuine creativity of abstraction: after all, are not the rebels for the underdog? And has not the system failed to bring about that justice which so clearly derives from its principles?

One might reply that it is not being for the underdog that matters, it is being for justice, and even though being for the underdog and being for justice often coincide, they do not coincide often enough to justify supporting the underdog and nothing else. Even more to the point is that intellectual and cultural development call for repeated applications of both associative fancy and abstractive discipline. The history of the development of civilization is the history of gradual *broadening of the frame of reference.* From the tribal man whose life was almost fully determined by the ties of blood—kinship and later caste—and whose ethos was limited in its application to those who were not strangers, mankind (or a great part of it) moved on to a phase in which the opinions of aliens were taken seriously enough not to be tolerated; this ushered in the era of missionary religions, in which the fate of a man could be transformed by conversion. Even though many a cruelty was applied to those who did not follow "the Faith," this was a broadening because at least all could accede to it and thus be granted the protection of law and morality. Later—now—we are approaching a stage in which the community of ethic no longer excludes tolerance for large areas of diversity. This is a further broadening of the frame of reference. As long as the nucleus of necessary laws is observed in action, freedom of thought is tolerated and even action is guaranteed. There are specific areas of personal choice to which the law does not apply. Contemporary man may think freely of things public and act freely in things private. But the maintenance or the improvement of this state of affairs requires clear abstractive distinctions between what is thought and what is action and between what is public and what is private.

However, this march toward more openness, this broadening of the frame of reference with respect to which man has to define his identity, was periodically interrupted by movements which, whatever might have been their original aim, led to a narrowing of the frame of reference, a restriction of the relevant to the in-group, and finally to bloodshed and destruction.

"Whatever might have been their original aim." The disparity between aim and result, the profoundly human desire and the inhumane practice, is brought out in the title of Norman Cohn's masterful study of such movements: *The Pursuit of the Millennium.*

The march of history is fraught with ambiguities: the aim appears sooner than it can be reached; there is disparity between goal and attainment; hopes are often betrayed by mistaken trials. The goodwill of urban renewal turns into the nightmare of Negro removal. Worldwide defense of self-determination turns into the quagmire of Vietnam. Why? Normal human incompetence or sinister conspiracy? Shall we sit down and analyze what it is that we did wrong, or shall we erupt in indignation? Shall we engage in the slow but productive process of abstractive examination, or shall we rise to the defense of our associative visions as if they were realities?

Vittorio Lanternari gave a partial answer to this question by selecting as title for his study, *The Religions of the Oppressed.* Patience comes more easily to the comfortable than to the disturbed. Ambiguity is greater, and anxiety stronger, for those whose need for answers is vital because their present status is uncertain. This means both the oppressed, social groupings in transition uncertain of their identities, and students oppressed by the double ambiguity of youth and of a profession the essence of which is finding—and knowing—the answers.

Yet the mere mention of such a double ambiguity is not enough to justify placing university students (more often than not representative of the overprivileged rather than of the average) among those practicing the escapism of the oppressed. Historically, it is from the semieducated lower-lower and lower-middle class that movements of associative reaction have drawn their strength. The confused have been among us before; it is not so long ago that (for example) they gathered in the Kingdoms of Father Divine—but the young intellectuals of the time paid little heed. It is only seldom, and only in periods of major cultural confusion, that intellectuals have taken up cudgels for the cause of anti-intellectualism.

But have they in this particular instance? Even in the privacy of my study I can *feel* the indignant objections with which the accusation is invariably met—and honestly, on the part of the objectors. Is not SDS a method of analysis, particularly suited, according to its tenets, for penetrating the hypocrisies under which middleclass society is hiding the Truth? The fact is that the one thing of which the New Left has proven itself completely incapable is to produce a single new idea. The Italian student who loudly proclaimed his mistrust of anyone over twenty-five did not even know that he was aping Mussolini. For that matter, direct and "natural" participation as a necessary basis of true democracy was the way in which fascist corporatism used to be justified. The best one can find by way of reasoning is a return to an extremely naïve version of Marxism–Leninism, including the thesis from *Imperialism, Last Stage of Capitalism* that the prosperity of the Western world, and in particular of the United States, is due to the exploitation of the colonies. However, what might be excused—or even admired—in the case of a man, Lenin—who perceived the failure of Marx's pauperization theses even before 1914, when this failure was far from obvious, and who tried to shore up Marxist theory by an appeal to profits drawn from the colonies at a time when balance of payments data were unavailable (the idea itself being hardly conceived)—is entirely impardonable in 1968, when (for example) anyone can read the data on the prosperity of the Netherlands after the loss of their investments in Indonesia, or on the continuous burden on the French finances resulting from France's remaining investments in Africa.

Nor is anarchy any more new than it is practicable. The closest SDS has come to novelty is in the fable that Germany was never Nazi, only obedient to a government which happened to be so: a historical falsehood invented *ad hoc* to justify civil disobedience.

Let us get back to the main point: it is only seldom, and only in periods of major cultural confusion, that intellectuals take up cudgels in the cause of anti-intellectualism.

There is one very important era when this did happen: during the era of Romanticism. To justify the opinion that Romanticism was anti-intellectual (despite its enormous artistic creativity) and to point out its kinship to the movement of 1968, I shall use words less suspect than mine, because they were written long before the fact; those of Irving Babbitt and of Laserre:

> The Rousseauist especially feels an inner kinship with Prometheus and other Titans. He is fascinated by every form of insurgency. Cain and Satan are both romantic heroes. To meet the full romantic requirement, however, the insurgent must also be tender-hearted. He must show an elemental energy in his explosion against the established order and at the same time a boundless sympathy for the victims of it. One of Hugo's poems tells of a Mexican volcano that in sheer disgust at the

cruelty of the members of the Inquisition spits lava upon
them. . . .   [*Rousseau and Romanticism*, p. 218]

With no more qualms than shown by the Inquisitioners themselves—who, after all, were earlier specimens of the same tendency,
and who, like all men convinced of their own goodness, dearly
loved their victims.

And again:

> Sublime convicts, idlers of genius, angelic female prisoners,
> monsters inspired by God, sincere comedians, virtuous courte-
> sans, metaphysical mountebanks, faithful adulterers, form only
> one-half—the sympathetic half of humanity. The other half,
> the wicked half, is manufactured from the same intellectual
> process under the suggestion of the same revolutionary in-
> stinct. It comprises all those who hold or stand for a portion
> of any discipline whatsoever, political, religious, moral or in-
> tellectual—kings, ministers, priests, judges, soldiers, police-
> men, husbands, and critics.   [*Le Romantisme Français*, p. 215]

This might have been the revolt of new wisdom against conventional wisdom—if it were ordered, if its rejection of the old were
a prelude to new insights, if its emotionalism were placed at the
service of understanding. But it is not. Fog, in the days of the
Enlightenment, was a nuisance. Within Romanticism, it becomes
an ever-present symbol: in poems, plays, paintings, it stands for
a blurring of boundaries, the suggestion of *something* beyond the
limits of vision: a suggestion paid for by making the vision itself
limited and unclear.

Yet Romanticism produced undeniably great art and undeniably
great poetry. Where it strayed beyond poetry and art, as in Germany, it led straight to Hitler. The reality, the unavoidability and
the manner of this evolution, were admirably documented by Kohn
and by Viereck.

The mechanism is simple: abstractive reason leads to a broadening of the frame of reference. It shows what men with differing personal experiences may have in common—even if it accomplishes
it at the cost of making impersonal that which it finds. Measure-

ment, scientific concepts, rules of law free of attempts at attainder are examples. The associative way is to accept as common only that which is also personal: unavoidably this means restricting the community to those with similar experiences, to exclude the alien. Worse: to mistrust it.

Idealism, self-righteousness, and paranoia may be merely coincidental. Faith in intuition, self-righteousness, and paranoia are not. Belief based on ratiocination or on empirical observation is always open to interpretation, discussion, the introduction of nuance, or correction. Belief based on intuition (except where used properly as a first step in a longer process) is faith. If it is evident to me, it is so, and should be evident to others; if it is not, they are blind or pretend to be.

For that, they must be either excluded from the body politic, and indeed deprived of any voice even in their own affairs, or else punished. Or both.

If I am bringing in Romanticism it is not so much to point to its consequences as to its origins. After all, Romanticism did not lead to Nazism everywhere—even though it strongly tended to, particularly in the form of the nationalism of many countries which might have acted as Germany did, if they had had the power. Nor am I suggesting that most of today's student romantics have the toughness and the insensitivity to become genuine fascists: the knownothings of the antifluoridation movements are likely to beat them to it.

Romanticism came about as a reaction against the extremely rapid cultural change brought on by the Enlightenment, and as a reaction to the cultural confusion which resulted from that change. Thus the origins of Romanticism—and this is the point— make it relevant to the movement of reaction against the extremely rapid cultural change brought about by liberalism and of reaction to the cultural confusion resulting from that.

The confusion at the end of the eighteenth century had many facets, each of which would take a library to describe. There was, for example, the equivocal role of France (particularly with regard to Germany): she preached equality in a language which was that of the upper classes, and fraternity by means of armies of occupation. Today we have the equivocal role of the United States: culturally aggressive and genuinely revolutionary—the image, understood or misunderstood, of American life and American products undermines customs, traditions, and loyalties all over the world—and at the same time politically defensive and conservative, because it understands that political stability is a prime need for genuine social and economic change.

The latter ambiguity (as the former) may be little understood, but it is often discussed. I shall therefore pass on, and take up something else: the ambiguity which at the onset of Romanticism and today surrounds the concepts of nature and naturalness.

Divinity and the legitimacy of monarchies having been dethroned, the energies of the Enlightenment had to be directed to Nature to find an arbiter between human egocentrisms. But nature —especially if spelled Nature—is a prime example of the basic antinomy to which all human knowledge is condemned: to feel natural, to let oneself go under the guidance of one's own nature, is incompatible with understanding nature, which calls for disciplined observation from the outside. We recognize the dilemma: between the associative and the abstractive, the subjective and the objective.

Let us couple this with another difficulty: that of the search for freedom. To feel free is—largely—to feel that one has a voice, perhaps a dominant one, in the shaping of one's own destiny. This calls for the fulfillment of two conditions: absence of external restraints (or their reduction to a tolerable level) *and* a good understanding of the world around. Let us insist on the second one: to act, one must know how and where; the one who does not know cannot act with the expectation that the outcome will correspond to the intent, ergo he cannot shape his destiny, ergo he cannot feel free.

The end of the eighteenth century and the middle of the twentieth were periods of sudden, almost explosive, removals of external restraints—with which the development of understanding did not keep pace.

The result is a feeling of unfreedom. And, since it is both easier and more natural to accuse others than to examine oneself, the feeling is attributed to the hypocrisy of a "system" which "pretends" to have removed external restraints, while "in reality" loading "its victims" with chains all the more heavy because they are invisible, hidden.

Paranoia, once again in history, is becoming the conventional wisdom.

An example: One of the sins of which "the system" West of the Brezhnev divide is most often accused is that of economic exploitation. The concept was unclear even at its inception more than a century ago; its use today, under conditions of truly extreme unapplicability, simply shows the also extreme dearth of ideas within the protest movement. If anything, the system should be accused of underexploitation: it is so productive, it needs so little human effort in its strictly economic sphere, that it leaves men or at least many men underexploited, that is to say economically irrelevant and psychologically unwanted.

This, indeed, is a social sin. The crucial point, however, is not the sin or even its seriousness, but the fact that the accusation does not fit it.

It is at this juncture that we come up against the question of why it is that today, as during the era of Romanticism, intellectuals take up cudgels in the cause of anti-intellectualism, which covers the more narrow question of the mutual relevance or irrelevance of the university and the revolution.

The role of the university (broadly speaking) is not to teach *what* to think, but *how* to think. Assuredly, the two can never be fully divorced, being tied together in what Dewey would call a transactional whole. Nevertheless the difference is easily perceptible, at least in many cases. This should make the university and the revolution mutually irrelevant, because revolutions are made in the name of the what, not of the how.

Or at least, this should make the mutual relevance of university and revolution tenuous—if the universities had been doing their job. Unfortunately, universities have been dissolving into welters of mutually irrelevant research projects and departments—teaching perhaps how to think in specialized branches of engineering, but not how to form *Weltanschauüngen*—views of the whole incidence of the world around us upon whole human persons. This is particularly true in the human sciences: the university teaches about a world of psychology, a world of sociology, a world of anthropology, one of political science and one of history—but not about a world of man. What is the meaning of science, not with respect to its objects, but as an expression of the human mind? What insights does the artistic vision contribute to science? Or, more generally, how does one think about a world in which a statesman's mistake may cost a student his life?

The usual answer to such a question—that it is not researchable —amounts to an abdication. Into the resulting intellectual void rush the half-baked: not knowing how to ask questions, they begin with answers. Not knowing how to examine the validity of statements, they take whatever *they* say as the voice of absolute virtue, and whatever differs from it as absolute vice.

The anti-intellectualism of the Romantic intellectuals was due largely to historical events beyond the influence of the community, which was then called that of the philosophers—but largely also to the sterility of late classicism, which had gone as far as it could in the domain of pure speculation and not yet caught up to the need of exercising intellectual rigor in the domain of observation. The anti-intellectualism—the fascism, to put it plainly—of the student rebels is due to a large extent to the fact that it is hard to consider as a misjudgment whatever impinges upon one's life—the war in Vietnam, or racial prejudice, or the incomprehensibility of the world around us, which are so much more easily called Crimes. It is also due to the sterility of a scholarly world which fails to see that the human need for synthesis cannot be indefinitely postponed for the sake of the rigor of analyses.

It is time to conclude. And in conclusion I must violate one of the holiest tenets of the system: the American rite of an upbeat ending. The prognosis, in my opinion, is bad.

One of the reasons for this is that the system has lost pride in its accomplishments. Even as wise and good a man as the late Adlai Stevenson said that you cannot inflame imaginations by the civilization of the supermarket; the more the pity, because that civilization stands for the resolution of a problem which had plagued mankind for centuries, that of the poverty of the working man.

Another—the major—reason for my pessimism has already been mentioned in a slightly different form. The decision-making processes in developed countries place real power neither in the people nor in any "power elites," but in the upper-middle echelons of a variety of bureaucracies. This, in effect, means that the decisions which impinge today upon the lives of people were made on the basis of the best conventional wisdom of yesterday. The reaction time of bureaucracies is slow; the way they act reflects the prevailing thought at the time of their recruitment, the time for moving up the ladder, the time for an involvement (Vietnam, for example) to ripen into its consequences. In a rapidly changing world, this is not good enough.

The point is not so much in the imperfection of the process—no government ever was or ever will be perfect. It is rather in the prosaic image of fate where fate is made up of briefcase-toting, honest but not holy, intelligent but not omniscient human beings. One can submit to fate only where its image is that of something bigger than human, ineluctable. Such as Self-Righteousness.

This is why our young "intellectuals" are grasping for the naked power of dictatorship.

They will not get it. Not because they are ignorant, unaware of the shoddiness of their hand-me-down ideas, but because they are not ignorant enough. The race for charisma goes invariably to the common denominator. Romanticism may have been ushered in by a Schlegel, but it took power through a Hitler.

BAD DAY AT GENERATION GAP

Glenn S. Dumke

The April 16, 1912, edition of the *New York Times* ran an interview with Captain E. J. Smith of the newly launched *Titanic*. Captain Smith made a point of the fact that ship-building had advanced to such a perfect art that absolute disaster involving the passengers on a great modern liner was quite unthinkable. ". . . I will go a bit further," he said. "I will say that I cannot imagine any condition which would cause this ship to founder. I cannot conceive of any vital disaster happening to this vessel."

Well, I don't pretend to have the foresight of Captain Smith, so I hesitate to make any sweeping predictions as to the seaworthiness of the academic ship-of-state. I don't believe it is yet time to man the lifeboats, but I have picked up a large obstacle dead ahead of us and unless I read it wrong, it has the power to cause a vital disaster. At this point, let's just call it partially surfaced public opinion. It is emerging, and it could be dangerous.

Two hundred million Americans are receiving almost daily psychic shockwaves via their television screens. Slowly, but surely, they are coming to two dramatic realizations. First, they have spent an enormous amount of money on higher education, which has become an economic and social necessity. Second, they are now quite aware that there is a youth revolution going on and that it seems to be headquartered on our college and university campuses. The so-called "good old days," when affluent parents sent their sons and daughters off to college "until they grew up," are now nothing more than a nostalgic memory. Colleges and universities in this country and around the world are bubbling and boiling, and there are many who are afraid that what is cooking is a witch's brew.

The instant electronic-communication medium which is largely visual in impact rather than oral has made little hilltop colleges in Ohio, Mississippi, or Oregon branches of what can now be called the "American International University." There has always been a community of faculty scholars that knew no campus, state, or national boundaries, but today, thanks to television, radio, and the press, there is also a similar community of students. When a student drops a pebble in the academic waters of San Francisco State, resultant waves lash up on the shores of Columbia or Brandeis. Thanks to instant replay, George Murray, Mark Rudd, Danny the Red, Tom Hayden [student and/or New Left leaders—Eds.] and many another name familiar to all of us are students in absentia in the American International University—not Berkeley, Wisconsin, or Paris. Thanks to the effectiveness of our mass media, Acting President Hayakawa, at San Francisco State, has become a national folk hero. Not only has television created international notoriety for countless student leaders, but it has taught a number of others their language, their dress, their style. There is little doubt in my mind that there is a direct relationship between the escalation of violence on our college and university campuses across the country and the saturation fixation television seems to have had on all types of violence—on and off the campus.

When public officials are invited to our campuses and then subjected to physical and verbal abuse, that makes news—not good news, but news. Students on every college campus across this country witness this new style of confrontation politics and many of them no doubt say, "Why not here?"

There are thousands of students on college campuses these days who are learning to be adept, skillful, practical politicians. They know how to analyze political, social, and institutional structures in order to find points of vulnerability. They know how to organize, attack, fall back, and regroup. They know how to get to the press and the TV media. They have learned that it is sometimes more effective to communicate with their college president via the Huntley–Brinkley Report than to make an appointment to see him in his office. The Gallup Poll reported in March of 1969 that campus disorders had replaced the Vietnam war as the primary topic of serious conversation in American homes.

A significant influence in the lives of this generation of young people is the fact that in all of their formative years they have grown up on a daily diet of violence brought into their home via television. It seems to be an axiom of television that violence makes news and news sells soap, so let's feature violence. The net effect is that our young people have been programmed for violence. Why shouldn't it be natural, therefore, for many of them to think of violent solutions to problems when they have seen hero after hero save the territory, save the bank, save the ranch—yes, save the world from the "bad guys" through violent acts of heroism? Indeed, I sometimes wonder how this generation was ever able to adopt peace or love as their verbal talisman under such circumstances. Perhaps it's a negative reaction.

I don't wish to oversimplify our problems and place all of the blame on television, for today's student is a product of a far different environment than most adult nonstudents knew. When my generation tries to tell the younger generation "like it really was" in the great depression, they simply ho-hum. Very few college students these days have ever wanted for anything. Compare the situation described in a recent college newspaper (that came across my desk) with what my generation experienced in the '30s. The head of the work–study program at this particular college was encouraging students to make up their own jobs on campus and then come in to his office for financing. Whereas most of us who wanted campus jobs had to haunt faculty offices, cafeterias, or head custodians day after day in order to press our needs upon them—if we were lucky, we got some help with meals or a room—and if we were really fortunate, we got on the payroll at 25 or 30 cents an hour.

The fact that many young people these days have little regard for security and material things shouldn't surprise us either. Few of them have ever been without them. They are more concerned about the quality of life they will have, not getting a job—that's the easy part of it. Recruiters come to the campus in droves, promising starting salaries that are often higher than those paid to professors.

When we try to tell this generation how the free world fought for its very life in World War II, and how after the conflict we expended our energies and our resources to rebuild the war-devastated nations—giving them back their territory, their national pride, and self-determination—their response frequently is, "That's very interesting, but what have you done lately?"

When we compare our efforts to prevent the Communist world from imposing their totalitarian form of government on smaller nations, their reply is likely to be, "But the Vietnam government is corrupt," or, "But Greece is ruled by a military dictatorship." In other words, if it isn't perfect and pure we shouldn't have had anything to do with it.

When we administrators say that we are opposed to separatism in our Black Studies programs or in our dormitories, they say, "You're inhibiting the development of ethnic identity and racial pride."

When we say every society since man first began to huddle together in caves has had their god and a religion, they say, "God is dead, and each man must control his own life."

When we say that we want to fight poverty, they say, "Stop the war in Vietnam first."

When we say we believe in free speech, democratic principles, and individual rights, they shout, "Power to the People"—all the while ignoring the fact that without a system of laws the people have no power.

When we say we want and encourage student participation in academic governance, they say, "Through subtle and devious means you're trying to make us part of the Establishment." As one student editor put it, "In forming the façade of partnership with the administration, the students have not realized the consequences of their act, nor have they been aware of the price they pay. The administration has crucified the students on a cross of responsibility."

When we say every individual should be held responsible for his actions, including arrest and trial for planting bombs, they say, as a San Francisco BSU [Black Students Union] leader did recently,

"The injuries to Tim Peebles (who had a bomb explode in his hands as he was planting it in a locker) were the fault of President Hayakawa and Governor Reagan, because of the suppressive atmosphere created on the campus by them."

Yes, it's a bad day at generation gap!

If I can believe my mail, there is a growing feeling among society at large that many professors and students regard themselves as part of a special-interest group free to exploit the rest of the community economically, socially, and morally. Traditions and values this society has revered and honored for hundreds of years are now under attack, on and off the campus, and people are worried. At no time in recent history has there been such a stirring among students and young people generally for change. This generation is impatient with the imperfections in our social order. Our very best products of urban, middle-class affluence are telling us that there is an awesome gap between the values we profess and the subversion of those values by our institutions and our bureaucratic society. Without increased efforts on both our parts to gain insights and mutual understandings, this gap is going to grow to a point where it is an unbridgeable gulf. That is a tragedy we simply cannot let happen. We are married to our students—there *is* no university without them. We may not divorce them and live a life of celibacy, for we have promised to love and honor them "in sickness and in health 'till death do us part." Unfortunately, the grim reaper is coming in the form of repressive legislation rather than graduation.

More than seventy-five separate bills dealing with control of campus disturbances are currently pending in the two houses of the California Legislature. A special Assembly committee has been named to probe campus disturbances. Our State Senate recently adopted, by overwhelming margins, "get-tough" legislation which in the words of their author "bring under control the activity of the radical–militant revolutionaries who are seeking to use our campuses as a sanctuary to bring chaos to our society." One of these bills would require the mandatory firing of any State College faculty member found to have participated in a campus disruption, or to have attempted to do so.

Legislators in almost every state are considering bills on discipline of students as well as faculty. Even in states where there has not been open conflict and disruption on their college and university campuses, the publicity given disorders elsewhere is moving legislators to act.[1]

The Illinois Senate recently passed a bill that would cancel the State scholarships of rioting students. Without public hearings, the Wisconsin legislature approved a bill that would revoke State support and scholarships of students who block traffic or disrupt classes. A bill before the Missouri legislature would make it a felony for a faculty member to encourage student agitation. In Wisconsin, one legislator has proposed to end faculty tenure, and another would give the joint finance committee the power to suspend salaries of university employees "for reasonable cause." Wisconsin now draws about 30 per cent of its 24,000 undergraduate students from out-of-state. A bill has been introduced which would place a quota of only 15 per cent on this class of students. The University Regents have already adopted this as a policy goal to be reached by 1975. This action provoked a protest by thirty-six academic department chairmen who called the action "a punitive response."

Wisconsin Regents have themselves been under fire from the Legislature. The majority leader of the State Senate has hinted of changes in the structure of the Regents "if they don't use their full authority" in dealing with campus militancy. He pointedly noted that the Regents were disbanded by the legislature thirty years ago in a political squabble.

A real danger is the escalation of violent reaction at both ends of the political spectrum and the resultant polarization of life on campus and in the community—the Right against the Left—the Third World against the administration—the faculty against the

---

[1] Numerous state legislatures have been in the process of passing laws to curtail campus demonstrations while overlooking the causes. A student who is convicted of inciting a riot on campus may be sentenced to up to ten years' imprisonment in Oklahoma, lose state financial aid in California, or in South Carolina face immediate expulsion following a hearing. And now the House Internal Security Subcommittee is conducting its own investigation of campus unrest. See "Students: The Legislatures React," *Time* (June 13, 1969), p. 58—Eds.

governing board. All too often honest differences of opinion are misconstrued to be deliberate and malicious attacks and obstruction.

Student protests are kind of like sin—you're either for them or against them. Right now, most people are against them. Our mutual task is to convince the controlling majority of students, faculty and the public that, as Thomas Mann put it, "The cure for an ailing democracy is more democracy." But we have to work ever so much harder at making democracy work. The psychologist William James spoke of "the secret and glory of our English-speaking system" which he said consisted of "nothing but two habits." "One of them," he continued, "is the habit of trained and disciplined good temper towards the opposite party when it fairly wins its inning. The other is that of fierce and merciless resentment toward every man or set of men who break the public peace."

At this critical time in history it is not good enough to stand on the sidelines and let a few students and faculty members, who regard themselves as part of a new-wave, intellectual, elite possessed by personal private insights, remain immune to the just laws of our academic society. If we do not act to govern ourselves, they could bring about the destruction of the one institution which has within it the intellectual, technical, and philosophical base which can develop corrections for our current social and political ills.

In spite of our mutually contingent relationship with the public, we have yet to work out a satisfactory system of checks and balances which will make us less vulnerable to destructive attacks, from within or without. On the one hand, we need to examine the conventional and traditional roles of trustees, faculty, students, and administration in the hope that such critical explorations will lead us to new, more effective systems and relationships better able to cope with the fundamental challenges each constituency faces daily in the arena of confrontation politics. On the other, we must open new avenues of communication with a much broader public than we once thought necessary. Higher education has suddenly become everybody's business.

We have made government, business, the military, and social progress dependent upon the skilled manpower, the technology, and the intellectual capacity represented in our institutions. In spite of this, there are many citizens and a few politicians who seriously toy with the idea of punishing us by withdrawing support until peace, calm, and "a proper respect" for the Piper who's paying the bill is evident on our campuses.

I sense an uneasy feeling among academicians, these days, about what should be learned and how it should be taught. Much of the former self-confidence and doctrinaire attitude displayed by faculty curriculum committees is gone. This is all to the good. Many of us are honestly searching for new ideas, new methods, new techniques which will break the lock-step conformity which has dominated our thinking for years. We are concerned about our particular institutions to be sure, but we are also concerned about the larger community which desperately needs our help.

I don't believe that any institution, such as Columbia, Berkeley or San Francisco, which has experienced a violent confrontation with student activists will ever again be the same. Such demonstrations, even if the issues are manufactured rather than real, shake our institutions to their very foundations. Some reform inevitably follows.

Many of the criteria which we have revered for so very long in higher education are nothing more than self-fulfilling, self-serving prophecies. Let me joust for the moment with just one of them. Essentially what we seem to have been saying is: give us your very brightest college applicants and we will give you high rates of persistence, superior academic performance, acceptance at the most prestigious graduate schools, and an impressive number of Woodrow Wilson Fellows. Why does Coach John Wooden at UCLA have winning basketball teams? He says it's because of his recruitment of superior talent. Go get the Lew Alcindors, the Curtis Rowes, the Sidney Wicks—they'll make you a contender in any league. But what about the boys who don't bring "seven feet" of high grades and test criteria with them to the admissions-screening board? Can we "coach" them into superior performance?

It is possible to adjust our programs to the student more than we have been doing without sacrificing the integrity of our academic programs. Let me cite just one example. In the 1968–69 Fall Semester, San Jose State College brought 195 "nonqualified" students into its Educational Opportunity Program. At the end of the semester,

72 per cent of these students had earned a grade-point average of
2.0 or better. Twenty-eight of this number achieved grade-point
averages of 3.0 or above, and two students earned straight A's. Of
the entire 195 students, there were only 7 withdrawals. Did this
performance take superior teaching, individual programming, and
a lot of personal motivation? Certainly it did!

Our whole concept of higher education has been based on the
concept that the rich get richer and the poor get poorer. The "best"
schools, with the "best" faculty, with the best student-teacher
ratios, with the best support budget get the best students. I think
it makes very sound educational sense, as well as social sense, that
we are finally challenging our best institutions and our best teachers
to see what they can do for "the least of ours."

Every college or university that has experienced a major confrontation has found its existing structure of academic governance
wanting. The decision-making process is too slow, too cumbersome,
and often not truly representative. Key faculty and administrative
committees have frequently been dominated by academic political
hacks. Academic senates, before the crisis situation, frequently had
great difficulty in getting a quorum, so that important and far-rang-
ing decisions were often left up to an executive committee. Most
of the work carried out by such machinery was done behind closed
doors, so that neither the students nor the general faculty had a
clear understanding of the positions or the issues at stake. The
faculty, as individuals, have surrendered virtually all of their institutional obligations, except the polite debate carried on over lunch
at the faculty club, to some remote committee, council, or "the
people up there," meaning the administration. The faculty collec-
tively controls the curriculum and instructional practices of all academic institutions. It is the faculty that sets the tone and character
of the educational environment. Presidents, deans, and other administrators are, to a large degree, effectively isolated from the seat
of real academic power—the faculty. If there is to be institutional
renewal, this is where it must take place; fortunately, there are now
serious signs of such stirrings.

I do not believe that the most serious danger to higher education
lies in the possibility that the violently militant students will take

over our institutions or generate outside our ivy walls any significant popular support for their "revolution." The real danger lies in the possibility that the momentum for improvement and change in our educational system, which has been generated by constructive, sincere activists and which is badly needed, will be diverted, blunted, and suppressed by a public mood which is repressive and vindictive.

How, then, can we provide a rational, effective defense of the collegiate establishment—not as it now exists, but as it might be? Criticism and protest is the easy way—for students or for administrators. Reform demands time, energy, constructive thought, and a large measure of good will. We are seriously short of many of these qualities right now, but in the words of Isaiah, "Come let us reason together."

Let's start by admitting that authority which rests solely on position, rank, or title is largely bankrupt. Why can't we give meaning to our words when we say a university is a community of scholars? This would mean that instead of suppressing student activists we would help them from becoming revolutionaries by working with them to clarify their goals and then, to the degree that these objectives can be accommodated within the mission of the university, helping them to achieve them. This would mean that we would have to involve students more than we are now doing in the operation of our institutions. The result would inevitably be a true community effort to find meaningful solutions to such problems as size, monolithic rigidity, depersonalization, and "relevance" which are plaguing us these days.

Why can't we gain a better understanding of our surrounding civic communities, and they of us, if we take the university into the community? I'm thinking of really massive expansions of student tutorial programs in our urban ghettos, internship programs, work semesters for credit, and practical student and faculty involvement in solutions to community, government, and social problems.

Why can't we develop new models for the intellectual transactions which go on between a student and knowledge—knowledge via a live teacher, a video-recorded teacher, a teacher in print, or a teacher which is a group experience on or off campus.

Our colleges and universities desperately need the free spirit and idealism of young people. It is only when the concerned and idealistic majority finds the door closed that the revolutionaries and the destroyers take over.

Yes, it's a "bad day at generation gap," but I have faith that it's not too late. In my judgment, the activist—not the terrorist—leaders of the current youth movement will not be destroyed for two reasons. One, it's simply impossible—they have much support from the majority of our talented, thinking, sophisticated students. And, second, because we will shortly come to the realization that it is important to our own institutional well-being to keep our critics alive, active—and most important, hopeful of progress and change within our democratic system. We may yet build a bridge of understanding between our generations—let's start by working from both sides.

EVENTS AND ISSUES OF THE
COLUMBIA REVOLT

Mark Rudd

Let me discuss the Columbia University revolt [of spring 1968] by briefly listing in order the major events: (1) the demonstration on April 23, (2) the occupation of the buildings, (3) the bust, (4) the period of the strike after the bust,[1] (5) the occupation of the building on 114th Street by the community during which about a thousand students were outside supporting them, (6) the second occupation of Hamilton Hall where kids went into the building because four people had been suspended, and (7) the ceremony where we held our own graduation. Those were the main events.

The issue of the gym[2] was one of the most important issues of the student strike, not only because we and the people of Harlem felt the gym itself was segregated and was an insult to the people of Harlem, but because the gym was also symbolic of the whole way in which the university faces the community—its exploitation of the community. To be more specific, Columbia, as an institution, had the policy of clearing out blacks, Puerto Ricans and other "un-

---

[1] On April 23rd, Mark Rudd led approximately one hundred students to Morningside Park to protest the proposed construction of a University gymnasium. After dispersal by the police, students began occupation of Columbia University buildings. Occupation was ended by the first police "bust"—arrest —on April 27. This was followed by a general student strike. Meanwhile a transient hotel at 114th Street was occupied by citizens of the Harlem community after Columbia announced plans to convert the building into University housing. The administration attempted to break the student movement by suspending four of its leaders, including Mark Rudd. The student answer was a second occupation of Hamilton Hall. During commencement, the movement held its own ceremonies—Eds.

[2] The gym, which was to be constructed in Morningside Park, would have taken over park facilities used by the black people of Harlem—Eds.

desirables" from Morningside Heights. We believed this policy of expansion into the community and the policy of removal of people to be racist. The gym was representative of this.

Another issue was IDA, the Institute for Defense Analysis, and the fact that Columbia has ties to it.[3] They do much research for the Pentagon into weapons systems, including counterinsurgency weapons systems like the electronic fence between North and South Vietnam, the McNamara line that was never built. That was developed by IDA with some professors from Columbia. Columbia is an institutional member of this, just like The American University is a member of the CRESS project on counterinsurgency warfare and area studies.[4] We wanted to stop IDA. We wanted to stop this support of the war and of the policy of imperialism—the entire American foreign policy.

The IDA issue was also symbolic—symbolic of all the ties between the university and the federal government. We were saying, through this issue, that the university has to stop supporting this imperialist foreign policy. We also demand that the School of International Affairs be abolished. The School does area-studies research; trains people for the CIA and the State Department; and trains people for jobs in the corporations which invest overseas and dominate the economies of other countries. These are the two main substantive issues that were at stake. IDA and the gym were two of the six demands.

Another demand was amnesty [for the student protesters]. We said that amnesty was preconditional to negotiation of the other is-

[3] The Institute for Defense Analysis contracts Defense Department research to its member universities. In addition, IDA employs research fellows at its headquarters near the Pentagon—Eds.

[4] The Center for Research in Social Systems (CRESS), formerly SORO (Special Operations Research Office), of the American University does contract research for the Department of Defense. CRESS' Army mission is "to conduct empirical and theoretical research, and provide information storage, retrieval and analysis services with a multidisciplinary orientation on social and cultural problems related to foreign areas of relevance to U.S. government programs." For further information on CRESS see James Ridgeway, *The Closed Corporation, American Universities in Crisis* (New York: Random House, 1968), and Irving L. Horowitz, *The Rise and Fall of Project Camelot; Studies in the Relationship Between Social Science and Practical Politics* (Cambridge: M.I.T. Press, 1967)—Eds.

sues because (1) we could never negotiate with these people when they had a club over our heads and (2) we felt they would use punishment to attempt to stop the political movement that we had built. They would throw the leaders out of school and put the rest on probation, so if we ever took political action again, we would be thrown out of school or busted again. We couldn't allow this to happen to our political movement. (3) The granting of amnesty was the recognition by the university that what we did had to be done—in other words, that we were right. We didn't think we were wrong in doing what we had to do, and we didn't think that any change could ever come about within the university until the Administration and the trustees realized that what they had been doing was wrong. Why should we be punished for doing what was right? We have not been told why and we have been punished. No real change has come about in the university except the change in people's heads—radicalization. And that's a very important goal.

The Role of the Faculty

After the bust, some faculty supported the strike because they were shocked by the cops, because they were shocked by the administration and thought Kirk [President Grayson Kirk—Eds.] was a bumbling idiot, or, in the case of a few, because they wanted to seize power for themselves and leap into the breach when the administration had lost all authority and all legitimacy. A few were really convinced that what we were doing was right all along and that even our tactics had been vindicated. An indication of this was that sixty people signed a petition supporting amnesty for the students. Amnesty was really the question that divided the men from the boys about what we were doing. The senior faculty got together right after we went into the buildings, held the first meeting they had ever held in the history of Columbia University, and gave support for Kirk. Up to that time, Kirk had done nothing. Then some liberals on the faculty signed a pledge that if the cops were to come, if the administration used any means of force against the students, they would interpose themselves between the cops and us and would join the strike. About a hundred of them signed and started an organization called the Ad Hoc Faculty Group which grew to about three or four hundred. These were the people taking an energetic role in things. Their line was that they would mediate between the students and the faculty—a basic liberal conception: if there's a problem, you work it out; both sides have equal truth, you just have to come together and resolve the conflict.

Behind this they had another basic liberal conception of themselves and of the university, namely that they needed peace and quiet to continue their weapons research, conflict resolution, politics or government or whatever lies they happened to be teaching. They wanted peace and quiet and they didn't want kids coming and bringing the outside world into the university. Although they were politically adept and their fields may very well have been government or sociology, they didn't understand what we were really out for—that we were really concerned with imperialism and racism.

They didn't understand that at times we'd be impolite about this or "intolerant" of the other side's rights (like the right of the university to keep expanding and keep throwing people out of their homes or their right to keep developing weapons for the Pentagon). They didn't understand that what we did had to be done. We tried to convince them, but they sided with the administration. Since they didn't side with *us*, they were on the other side. It was just that clear—they said that they were in the middle but politically they had to choose a side. If they didn't, they were on the side of the *status quo*. They were naïve in thinking that they could be in the middle and they were naïve in some of the things they did. For example, they put up a blockade around Low Library before the jocks [i.e., athletes] did it. They were the cops before the jocks were there. In addition, they were the people we had to fight the most. They would come round to the buildings, trying to scare people saying the bust was coming, the jocks were coming, beware of the right-wing reaction, time is of the essence, all of these phrases. Although they said they supported us, they weren't out for the same goals we were.

There were a lot of reasons for this. One is that the faculty is engaged in the process of transmitting lies from one group to another and the lies they tell, especially in the social sciences, are lies that help to perpetuate the *status quo*. Lies like pluralism and what economics is about in this country. Or else they teach the wrong stuff. If you're in economics, they don't teach you critical economics, they teach you how to do statistics so you can work for the Pentagon or for GM. Or, if you're in sociology you don't learn how to criticize the society: you don't learn about the roots of the society although you might learn about doing research into people's attitudes. It's complete ideology we get from our professors. And they're so committed to this garbage that they're not about to join a movement to overthrow the ruling class in this society because they believe in the things that they're teaching. They have to be committed to those lies or they'd have tremendous identity problems. That's why so few professors side with us. This is not "free speech," these are not "liberal" issues. We are involved in getting down to the roots of things.

Mark Rudd: A Personal Vision

I could stand here and recite a whole list of ills in this society. I could also give you some ideas I have about what a nice society would look like. I think it would be very abstract, but you can see already that some of the things that we're opposed to have to do with exploitation of people and that behind all of this we see, in this society, a ruling class. That's what the whole trustee bit at Columbia was about. We talked about how the ruling class uses Columbia.

People have written books on ideology and I can't give it a name, "socialism," "communism"—I really would rather not. Listen to what I say and maybe some of the things that I believe will come through. Living in this society, seeing how it's run, opposition to it, and opposition to racism, imperialism, and repression is very positive. If you're against repression, you're for freedom; if you're against racism, you're for a society in which people treat each other as human beings. I have certain ideas about the way society could be, and I know that our goals at the moment are developing a mass democratic socialist movement.

I know that any blueprint I wrote for the institutions in a socialist society would either be unworkable, utopian, or else I'd become a Stalinist, to force people into the blueprint. So, I think that the democratic institutions will be determined by how we make the revolution. The thing we're looking for now is the development of a mass democratic, political socialist movement. The movement can be defined in terms of being against racism, being for national liberation in the third world, being against the system of capital and private profit. To the people fighting for their freedom in the third world, it doesn't matter if the president of the United States is Eisenhower, John Kennedy (who was responsible for the Bay of Pigs), Johnson, or even McCarthy (who said he would stand up to communism in Thailand). Liberal policies are as bad as the conservative policies.

The Function of the University: Enlightenment or Expediency?

I think you're making a fundamental error when you define the interests of those who rule the University in terms of their economic profit. You're a vulgar Marxist if you do that because some of these guys are not making strict economic profit off the University. Just getting people socialized to take a role, filling a slot in the society, even that serves the interests of the ruling class. And that's very different from direct economic profit. We don't want to be vulgar Marxists about it. The way that the University is set up with a professor who stands giving you the line, orienting you toward a hierarchical relationship, is itself very helpful to the ruling class. Also, the ideas that are taught are extremely important. The lie about the governmental process, about pluralism, groups working out their interests being represented in the final decisions, is not the way the government works. That's the theory of pluralism and that's not the way things go.

The functions of the University are very intricate: they turn out personnel. IBM puts a million and a half into Columbia School of Business; it gets out of it a program in international marketing. The State Department or the CIA gives x amount of money to Columbia School of International Affairs and they get out of it a piece of data about the national income of Czechoslovakia.

Now let's try to look at the University for enlightenment. Columbia students re-evaluated their lives. They re-evaluated what we had been saying about imperialism and racism. They identified with the oppressed of this world, the Vietnamese and the blacks, and they joined the movement. Their lives were changed. I would like to see us develop a university that has a critical function. Except for the radical students, universities don't promote real change.

The System: Possibility of Change
from Within

Even if we were assured that one can change the foreign policy of the United States from the inside and that one can actually learn about the foreign policy of the United States at a university, foreign-service schools train people who don't want to change foreign policy. These institutions are even more dangerous because, as in the case of the Russian Institute at Columbia, rationalizations are developed for things like the Cold War. Moreover, people have been trained there for use in Cold War institutions like the Free Europe Committee, the State Department, and the CIA and Radio Free Europe. I also know that the ideas there are used by people predominantly to perpetuate this system. They develop more and more sophisticated means of controlling the people of Peru at the Latin American Institute at Columbia. Knowledge, however, can be used on both sides. We had Anthropology Department people, radicals, who decided they wanted to help the liberation movement in Peru. They did research into the social structure of Peru, but they realized that their findings could be used equally well by the State Department and by the military for repression of the liberation movement in Peru.

I don't agree with the assumption that one can change the system from the inside. To think that you're going to change a foreign policy that's based on the interests of the ruling class in the society by working for the State Department, and to think that these foreign policies don't have a political basis as well as an economic or class basis, is crazy. I think the way that we've got to change foreign policy is through a mass movement of people re-evaluating this country and its goals, as well as their own goals. The masses would then oppose the war in Vietnam not because it was an accident, and not because the United States is getting whipped, but because it's imperialist and it doesn't serve their interest at all. It hurts their interests. We're doing our own analysis of this country, and we have to go outside of the institutions of repression which exist in order to do it. Now if you're interested in changing the foreign policy, why don't you join us? You can work through research; you can work with other committed people who are studying problems; you can also work to develop a mass movement of people committed to changing the foreign policy of the country. That's the only alternative I can see. I want us to develop a university that has a critical function.

The Future of the Movement

The issues we raise are not predominantly student-oriented. They have to do with the relations of the university to the rest of the world. Our question now is how to broaden out the student movement and to bring more working-class people, people in the community, and black people to that same kind of radical understanding of the society that we have. Basically, the campus is highly politicized and people are at the point where they understand the issues in general. We're now going to talk in specific terms about these different things, these viewpoints that we've raised. The student movement must now relate these specific tactics and viewpoints to the world. It must become an agent for change in a worldwide arena.

THE BLACK UNIVERSITY

Ewart Brown

I want to say something about the Black University and the black student revolt, so to speak. For the past year or so, there has been a great deal of publicity given to the concept of a Black University. Needless to say, as is the case when the word *black* is used anywhere, there is a great deal of questioning, a great deal of surprise among many people because we have not yet reached the point where we can accept the word *black* placed before any idea or included in any concept. And so, when Nathan Hare[1] and other people started talking about the Black University as fertile ground for the operation of the Black Power philosophy, people began to seriously question the sanity of the people who were talking about it. But after going through various stages of student protest and revolt, etc., I've come to the conclusion that the Black University is exactly what we all need—that goes for black students, white students, and every other type of student. We need a Black University primarily because the Negro University has failed, as has the Negro concept. And I'm not trying to involve us in a battle of semantics, but I think before we discuss seriously the situation, we have to make clear a line of distinction between the Negro and the black: It's a fact and we have to establish this distinction so that when we talk about the Black University, you are within a perspective that allows you to speak, as Malcolm X said, "Intelligently instead of unintelligently." Now the concept of the Negro University has been at-

[1] Dr. Nathan Hare was formerly Professor of Sociology at Howard University. He is author of *Black Anglo-Saxons* and acting chairman of the Black Studies Department at San Francisco State College—Eds.

tempted or has been worked upon by many, many so-called institutions of higher learning, Howard University being one. The Negro
University is the institution that has arisen because of the effects
of racism. It is a reaction. It did not grow out of creativity. It did
not grow out of any concern or constructive plans of black people.
Howard came into existence because black students could not go
anywhere else—or, at that time, Negro students could not go anywhere else. And so the concept of the Negro University actually
came to mean to us a place of refuge, a place where we could go
together, forget what we are, a place where we could sit and talk
about parties and Cadillacs and Corvettes and forget about true
education.

And so we find that the Negro University, of which Howard is an
outstanding example, has contributed greatly to the perpetuation of
the racist ideology. And without even recognizing it, we have made
this contribution. Whereas the Black University now, as I see it,
would destroy all these negative concepts, these negative ideas
about what black people are. It would completely obliterate the
Negro concept. It has to do more with destruction of the self-
hatred that we have for ourselves and building of respect and a sort
of establishment of a fortress center of Afro-American thought and
education. So by Black University, we obviously mean that the institution is going to dedicate itself to the solutions of the problems
that black people have. And I would guarantee that if I ask the
question of ten people, if I said, "What do you think about a Black
University?" I guarantee that the reaction from 90 per cent would
be, "Well, does that mean that you can't have any white students?"
And that is exactly what we are dealing with. That is the slave mentality, the mentality of dependents. We cannot have anything of
our own unless somebody white is in it. And this is the idea the
Black University would destroy. The Black University would have
a concept that says, "This is a Black University, period."

I conducted an informal survey at Howard earlier this year, and
I asked about 100 people in the Medical School different questions
about their undergratuate education. And I would ask people,
"Well, did you go to Howard?" and they'd say, "Well, I went to a
white school." And it came out so smoothly. No one even asked

any questions. No eyes open wide. They went to a white school. It's all right to talk about a White University, it's accepted as is everything else white is accepted in this country and many other countries. But when we speak of a Black University, we begin to allow the self-hatred idea to the surface, the dependence, the idea that we cannot do anything, we cannot construct anything unless there is a white person involved in the construction. And people say that this is racist—"reverse racism" is the phrase that they use for it. They say White Universities are letting black students in now, and that's progress. Well, we would start off letting anybody who wants to come into the institution come in, so that we wouldn't have to call that progress. It would be a Black University, a center of Afro-American learning, learning about ourselves, learning about other people than those in Western countries, learning about everything that has brought black people to the present situation. In history classes, for instance, we would try our best to gather material written by historians rather than history writers, and I'm sure you know the distinction. In economics, we would begin to deal with concepts other than capitalism, we would begin to question every present economic system and find out whether there are alternatives to the present one, which doesn't seem to be doing too well for black people, and other minority groups for that matter.

And so the Black University would be an institution dedicated to the solution of the problems of black people, as I believe all black institutions should be dedicated. The black community has many problems, and we know that the overall cause of the situation is racism, but we can't base an institution on the concept of destruction of racism as such. I think before we do that, we have to base it on where we are now. And I think that is what is important, and hence we find students screaming across the country for the establishment of Black Studies programs and sometimes I sit down and think about that. It's all right for white schools—maybe that's as far as it will go in white colleges anyway. But I am sort of leary about the establishment of Black Studies programs in universities that are trying to become black. Nevertheless, being practical, I have to realize that Howard University, for instance, is maybe nearly as white as Duke, philosophically speaking. And so, in order to get a foothold, we might have to establish Black Studies programs in our Black Universities, to our disgrace, of course. But we have to start somewhere. This is what people are saying today—we have to start with something tangible within the university. But I would like to see some time later a situation where we don't have to set aside a little school for niggers over in the corner and call that the Black Studies program. We want to make the entire university oriented so that there is no need for a special program, so that if it is a Black University it produces a black thing, and so that people who come out of the university don't have to have a degree in Black Studies. This is what I'm most leary of—where people are going to know all of black history, they are going to know everything about black people and leave the university and go out on Wall Street and join the entire system there. And I think that this is where we have to be very, very careful, and what we must try to avoid.

As a Black University, Howard is going to have to make the transition from dependence on government to one of independence. I think that we can do that if we give the black people—both those who go through the institution and those who don't have a sense of community—a sense of belonging to that institution. I'm saying, for instance, that a graduate of Howard would have no problem whatsoever in providing a portion of his income for that institution. We took a survey at Howard two years ago and found that in a period of ten years, the average alumni contribution was $2.91 per year. This is what we are talking about, people who leave Howard with such a poor taste in their mouths that they don't ever want to see that institution again. I believe that this in itself is an outgrowth of the Negro University concept. People don't *love* the institution—they *use* the institution. They don't feel they are a part of it and they don't feel they should help to maintain the institution as the years pass on. I think specifically that the graduates would have to come up with some money. Howard produces more black doctors, more black lawyers than any other institution in the country, and yet the Medical School is lacking in facilities and faculty. If we establish that love for the institution, the graduates will be able to take over the financing of the institution.

Howard has a good chance of becoming a Black University just like Federal City College, even while it gets its money from the Federal Government. The government has got to keep the people quiet, has got to keep the people calm. The government has got to maintain a few nigger universities, they have to, because if you don't have some nigger schools, then these black kids are going to want to go to the white schools—and you can't have a great influx of black kids into white schools. I mean, we'll take a few, so that we can take some pictures and show how much integration is here, but they don't want to have a whole influx of niggers into these schools. What I'm saying is that out of necessity, I think they'll say, "Well, hell, you know, what's a couple million dollars, just to let them do their thing on their own?" But I think that gradually it is going to come to a point where they realize that the products of these institutions are people who are out to destroy them in various aspects of their operation, and I think that that is when black people are going to be called on to support their own thing.

The Federal Government itself, practically speaking, is not anywhere near the ideal. And so everything that appears to be idealistic would naturally have to be, to some extent, antigovernment, and that is why they would become uptight. For instance, in the Black University, I could see courses on the various systems of government—not just learning them but, if they look better, trying to implement them. Now, that is an obvious threat to the *status quo*, and therefore, they would become uptight. They would become uptight because black lawyers coming out of Howard Law School and having done away with courses in international finance and having courses in welfare rights would begin to leave that institution and go out for the purpose of changing the situation.

The government becomes uptight because the government capitalizes on the ignorance of the black students who were, for so many years, trying to be white. All these things are tied in. There was no call for black history and black culture in these institutions.

I don't want to know about Frederick Douglass so I can run around the street quoting him. I want to learn about Frederick Douglass so I can have more insight. I want to know why things are like they are today. So then I become a threat to the *status quo*.

The Federal Government has fought to keep people, various segments of the population, black and white, subjected to their system, and in doing so they benefit—and I'm talking about individuals and corporations. Now the only way I can see our getting out from under this system is to use the institutions we have at our disposal and I think that white institutions also have to begin to structure their curricula and their various activities on the campuses to question the present situation, question it so that after the questioning you can delete certain inconsistencies and inadequacies. Then it is your responsibility, black or white, to work toward changing it in whatever way you see fit.

In making this Black University—or implementing any other change for that matter—it will not be easy, but I like to think it can so I can continue. I need some faith, I need some hope that it can be done and it is very easy to give up because there are people who have natural hair with processed minds. Let's consider the value of having natural hair. In any such struggle as this, we need symbols. Symbols are very, very important. Yes, some people do have arguments as to who has more dashikis or whose hair is longer—you know, we realize these things happen. But the mere fact that a guy has long hair and he is wearing clothes that symbolize something other than Western culture provokes thought. It makes a little kid ask his mother, "Mama, why does he have his hair like that?" She has to answer. And I say this because we have to stimulate thought; it is not necessarily an indication of what is going on in one's mind, but it helps. It helps because we have to have these signs of difference, signs of change, and we build upon that. Now I know that at Howard it is very difficult to change things, to make people realize that we ought to go somewhere that is common. But I am happy that there are changes.

In three of four years, Howard has changed tremendously. I'll give you an example: When my class came in September to the Medical School, an insurance agent asked us if we could come in and talk about insurance policies, as he'd been doing for ten years. The other students had already said how interesting the talk was because he definitely was telling doctors how they could make the best out of their lives. Well, he came in Monday morning and there were about eighty people there and he started off by saying, "Now, let me make one thing clear, I know you are here to learn medicine, but I know you have visions of that big house and that big Cadillac in the driveway. . . ." My class got up and walked out. I'm using this as an example of the change in the thinking of the students, not that they *won't* have a big car or not that they *won't* have a big house. But these things are no longer at the peak of the payment. I know I once was a Negro and I still have certain Negro behavior patterns—I know this—but we are all trying to change, and I think that, as Stokely [Carmichael] said, we have to eliminate the negative and accentuate the positive. And if we do that, we can keep it moving.

In the past three years the group at Howard that has probably provided more impetus than any other has been the freshman class. We used to have a course at Howard called Freshman Assembly which was organized because black students were culturally deprived and black students had to go to the auditorium every Tuesday afternoon and sit down and listen to Mozart or somebody else's symphony. So the freshman class last year decided it wanted no more of this and they disrupted one of them and there have been no Freshman Assemblies since. And this, I think, is an example of the change they undergo before they get into the institution. Now I was a junior before I even started digging myself for what I am. These guys are coming in as freshmen and these people realize already who they are. So if the institution presents them with anything negative, they are not going to stand for it. We find the guys who are sophomores or juniors today are pretty well clear on what they want to do, and it is displayed in the Medical School. It was unheard of for medical students to talk of boycotting classes and staying out until the demands are met, it was ridiculous. Of course, some of them say that this is my job and that I went to the Medical School on a mission impossible and that I had a specific job and that was to disrupt the Medical School. We have 106 people in our class and not one student broke the boycott for nineteen days. So I use this as an illustration of the change as we move along different levels of education.

I could see in the Black University a total breakdown in the distribution of power. First of all, I would hope that it would not be a corporation, I would hope that the institution could be run by some system that would allow trustees—or if you want to, call them moneymakers—who would go out and get money for the institution; but how the money is used would be decided by those people who actually live their lives there in the institution—students and faculty members. Administrators would act as hired hands subject to being fired when they do not make sure that the machinery that has been defined is in good working order. That's their only function. And the present system we have—presidents whose knowledge of the educational situation is limited and hampered by their efforts to go out and get money—is not good. President Nebrit of Howard has to go down to Congress with his hat in his hand and he has to try to get money for the institution, and in so doing he is obligated to deny the students a great deal of learning which they need to have. And so we have this conflict of interests, trying to get money and thereby limiting the scope of the educational environment.

The Black University would also have a strong connection with the community surrounding the college. The aims of the institution would definitely have to include some establishment of channels into the community and back, so that Howard students won't be looked upon as people that are a step further than the guy on 14th Street who wants to break his head open because he goes to Howard University. We have to destroy that concept in the Black University. We have to establish such rapport with the people in the community that they defend the institution whenever it needs to be defended, verbally and otherwise. And we have to have people who realize that the institution is there for them, and not for the 10 per cent of the black population that might have the money to go on to higher education. The community tie-in is very important because—as I said, it is sad to see—the values that graduates of Negro Universities have are disgraceful because they contribute to the attitude of that guy on 14th Street. The graduate of Howard's Medical School: for many years, the first thing on his mind was to go out and buy that big Cadillac.

So to implement all these things will take effort and time, and the question then comes up as to what effect this will have on the "law and order," for which Nixon and Agnew campaigned. The extent to which "law and order" is not observed will depend on the amount of tension that is in the atmosphere and the amount of response that comes from those who are being attacked. I don't think that students are particularly concerned about observing law and order—they want some changes. The law students at Howard surprised me when they gave up the building they had seized.[2] The usual course of action taken by administrators or people in power is to resort to the courts and to obtain a temporary restraining order. They did it last year when we went into the administration building. When you make that commitment, you should seriously consider what you are doing. The law students knew when they were going to take over that building that the administration would move in that manner. And it is ridiculous and it reflects poorly upon you when, after you take over a building the man comes with his restraining order and then you give the building back to him—you are right where you started. If you are going to use that as an ace card, hold on to it, don't let go. In the spring of 1968 when we occupied the Administration Building, on the second day, the administration got this court order and they sent us a telegram saying, "At 5:00 P.M. the U.S. Marshal will appear and he will read so and so and so and so and you will have to vacate the building." He came and read about two sentences and we told him, "No, leave, we don't want it, we are staying." You have to recognize the position you are in: Howard is located in a very strategic position as far as the city is concerned, and they

[2] Howard University law students occupied their law building in the Spring of 1969 to protest the lack of student participation in the decision-making process of the Howard Law School. When the administration obtained a court restraining order, the students vacated the building peacefully—Eds.

don't want any trouble. Last year it was around March 20, it was getting warm and people were getting restless—so why try to force students out of a building?

Nobody wants to see a thousand students being led into paddy wagons to go downtown. That gets sympathy. There is the possibility that one student might not like it and might try to hit somebody and then the cops beat him in the head and that is the start of a big thing. So, I'm saying, it depends on your degree of commitment as to whether you are going to become violent or not. If the situation brings it about, then you have no choice. They make all sorts of threats when you are in a position like that. I'm from Bermuda, and the first thing they told me was that "You can get deported, because if they have to come in here and take you out, and you've committed an offense, then you are subject to deportation." I think many students are resorting to violence because the possibility of communication is completely lost. The disturbance at San Francisco State, for example, was a military battle; that is what's going on. It is no longer a question of right-and-wrong and academic freedom. The major brunt of the thing is, Who will win and who will lose? The students are serious about their actions, and even if they ended them right now, they would be thrown out of school—so they say "why not blow up a building?" You've got to realize how serious these people are. Their whole attack now is removing people, and if the people don't move, they will move over them and try to move down some buildings. And this is what they are doing—they are destructively constructing something. The people in power don't listen and they don't believe that students will do this.

So all this is happening, and will continue to happen, and the Black University is going to exist. You cannot expect that someone who is supposed to look up to the doctor and up to the lawyer, and who sees the overt signs of making it—the big Caddy and the big house—you could not expect him to reject these values if he's being made to believe that this is everything that there is. And this is what the university is for. We are trying to redefine the values so that a black person going into a college will go realizing that in going to that institution he will come out a better black man, a man capable of looking at a situation and deciding how he is going to help apply the solution to that problem. And I know that many of these concepts sound general, but the concept of the Black University itself is young and there are many ideas and you might have some yourself. But I think the major job of the Black University would be: number one, to obliterate the Negro; number two, to detect, define the problems of the black community; and then from there, set up your departments or colleges as you see fit to move on these problems and use all manpower resources within the college to solve the problems of the black community.

A WORD TO STUDENTS

Eldridge Cleaver

I want to say that I'm very glad to be here, particularly because this is the capital of the United States of America, the pigpen of Babylon. I'd like to come through here in a Sherman tank. This is the place where mass murders are plotted against the people, where simple-minded motherfuckers like Lyndon Baines Johnson, Hubert Humphrey, Richard Nixon, and all these other political freaks enact their plots against the people. I say these politicians are enemies of the people because the entire government of the United States, all of the pigs of the power structure, are enemies of the people. They have forgotten that they are public servants—that they don't own the people. They are supposed to be carrying out a job for the people.

They want to make us believe that the people in the country have become impotent, that there's nothing they can do to move or control their own destiny, that, in fact, you have to leave it to buffoons like this racist pig from Alabama, George Wallace, or my home boy, bone-nose Nixon, and meat-head Humphrey. I don't know how many of you are going to vote in November, but I will tell you this: I am not here seeking votes. I am the Presidential candidate of the Peace and Freedom party, but it's only the visionaries in the Party who think that we are going to have a President in the White House this time around. As a matter of fact, if I were elected, I would not enter the White House. I would send a wrecking crew there to burn the motherfucker down. Then we could build a monument to the decadence of the past on the ashes that would be left.

There's never been a President in that building who has done his job or fulfilled his responsibilities to the people. There have been gangsters, criminals, and cutthroats in that White House and it needs to be abolished along with the political machinery in this country that allows them to wiggle their way into it. If you don't realize that, then you don't understand what's going on in the world today. You don't understand the task confronting your generation, and you aren't going to be able to deal with it when it's thrust upon you.

I come from a state where they have this place called Disney-land and we have a governor out there from Disneyland also, Mickey Mouse Reagan. You're probably familiar with him from having suffered through some of his grade-B movies. He recently did all of us a favor. There were a lot of people confused by him; they didn't know where he was at. But when the students at Berkeley offered to let me lecture in a course there, he ran out front and oinked in the face of the people. Now they see him for what he is—a racist pig who has nothing on his mind.

We have to start thinking about alternative ways of dealing with this political situation. Since the politicians have closed all the channels for redress of the people's grievances, we have to look at history for precedents. We have a very fine one that they call the Boston Tea Party. We need another Boston Tea Party from one end of Babylon to the other. I'm not talking about a tea party where white people put on Indian clothes and headdresses, then come out pretending to be dissatisfied. I'm talking about whites coming out in their own faces, with some real Indians there, black people, Puerto Ricans, and every other ethnic group in America, to protest. Not only to protest, but to take action. To drag the pigs of the power structure out by their ears and throw them into the garbage cans of history where they belong.

We say all power to all people. Black power for black people, white power for white people, red power for red people, brown power for brown people, yellow power for Mao Tse-tung, Ho Chi Minh, and all their brothers and sisters—whether the pigs in power like it or not. The oppressed people of the world are moving. They're not going to accept this shit any longer. As a colony within the mother country, the black American is here within the belly of the whale in Babylon to join forces with them, proud to take his place in the ranks of the revolutionary third world. And we ask all sympathetic whites to come out and help us liberate the people of the world.

I know that a lot of blacks get uptight when I say, "White power for white people." Someone asked me, "What's that you talk about, man, white power for white people? I mean, they been fucking over us all this time and why do you want to give them some more power—even talk about power for them?" But the point is that white people may think they've had power in this country, but they've had pig power masquerading in their name. I think that distinction is becoming more apparent. The people must be distinguished from the pigs.

I define the pigs as those actively involved in the oppression of people: the avaricious businessmen, the demagogic politicians, and the racist pig cops. Huey P. Newton, Minister of Defense for the Black Panther party, was the first one I ever heard use the word "pig." "Pig" in the American mind carries connotations of something low and sloppy. It looks like the police in this country are going crazy, doesn't it? Running around, killing people; they're acting like real pigs. Their behavior shows they have developed a caste-consciousness. They're motivated by patriotism: defending the borders of civilization against barbaric hordes, niggers from the ghetto—that's what they mean. So that's what they're into and they're the best organized group in the country. They have political machinery and are governed by the International Association of Chiefs of Police of which Chief Cahill, the police chief in San Francisco, has just been appointed head. Think about this merciless caste of knights in dull armor who are moving, who support Wallace, who support the military, who support the war, who oppose anything beneficial for the people, and who represent a standing army in their midst. A racist gestapo, a hostile force whose members have to be taught that they are public servants with no right to drive over the people.

The cops see themselves as a special-interest group. As a matter of fact, they are blamed for a lot of things they are not responsible for. But they are the guardians of the law and when the pigs in power tell them what the law is, whether it's the law or not, they will come down to enforce it with their guns, billyclubs, and Mace.

The word "pig" does not refer to all white people. We make a distinction between those of the power structure and those who are being oppressed, abused, and misused by the power structure and all of its arms and tentacles. The students here that have joined me are not the pigs.

I think white people have a right to speak out against the evils they see around them, even when the evil is in the black community, because whether you know it or not, whether you like it or not, it concerns you. It's your business, and that is why I feel perfectly justified in speaking out about what I see going on in the white community. There are a lot of misguided black people who are what we call cultural nationalists and they cry "racist" at every turn. You have to recognize that they have agents, and any time black people get together, they send a battalion of their agents to confuse the situation. One of their favorite methods is to use pseudo-black-nationalist rhetoric to mask counter-revolutionary motivations. We oppose that whenever it presents itself: we're not going to paint ourselves into a corner in order to be able to holler "black, black, black." We say blackness is essential, but it's not enough. After you learn that you're black you got to move beyond that to learn that you're oppressed and to learn who your oppressors are. You must be able to distinguish your oppressors from your friends or allies so that you know where to look for strength in jacking up the pigs in the power structure.

People today are either part of the solution or part of the problem. As far as I'm concerned, the press constitutes a large percentage of the problem because they are liars, distorters, and propagandists. They lie about people. They lie about students who demand changes in the university. The underground press is beginning to circumvent their monopoly and the grapevine will move past them. We have to recognize that one—if not the basic—problem in the country today is confusion—primarily because of the distortion, the lies, spread over radio and television, through the newspapers and magazines.

They put out a lot of lying propaganda about the Black Panther party. They say that the Black Panther party is a conspiratorial organization, and that it wants to drive through the suburbs and murder all the little white children. Well, this is part of their program of distortion, designed to perpetuate confusion so the people in America will look at each other as enemies instead of focusing on the true enemies of the people. When members of the Black Panther party are involved in violence, it's always a case of confrontation with the police. You won't find any instance of Party members in an altercation with people, just plain Joes and Johns, ordinary citizens of the community. But you do find us defending ourselves against those pigs who come into our community like an occupying army. They are there to protect the businessman's interests in keeping black people suppressed. We repudiate them, we want them out of our community, and we'll get them out with guns if we have to. Black people in America have lived under the gun every minute they've been here, and we want an end to that. The only way we can see to end it is to get their guns out of our community. We think we have a right to do that. They can take their guns back to the white community, if the white community will tolerate that, but get them out of our community.

We demand that those who police black neighborhoods must live there too. If they are going to brutalize us, then they must come in to sleep at night so we will know how to find them. Because when they brutalize us or shoot us, we are going to hang them. They need to know that. They need to know that just as the Jews hunted down Adolph Eichmann, we are going to keep a list ourselves and we are going to execute these pigs for crimes against the people.

Why is it that the followers of Hitler, Mussolini, and Tojo could be taken to places like Nuremberg and put on trial as war criminals? Well, the police are just as much war criminals as they are. These pigs are human-rights criminals guilty of denying the people life, liberty, and the pursuit of happiness. We've never really dug it, and we're just getting to the point where we know we don't have to go for it any longer. We won't miss this opportunity because it looks to us like we have genocide in store on the horizon with a pig like George Wallace running around.

The boot is kept on our necks through violence and we wish to pose revolutionary violence against it. The black people in this country are subjected to a form of colonialism and, just as in a colony abroad, we have all the apparatus of colonialism including the colonial administration and the standing army. The standing army to black people is the police, and we want to get them off our backs. But when we move to get them off they use their guns. So we have to get some guns and shoot back. We make no bones about it, we're not ashamed, we're proud of it, and we say, "All power to the people!" We're proud of our leader, Huey P. Newton, who set a very beautiful example by going out into the streets at night in the alleys with these racist cops, standing on the right to defend his people and telling these pigs that if they shoot at him he'll shoot back. We got to get into that because the pigs aren't going to relent.

Now, you ask, how can we survive with only 10 or 11 per cent of the population? This is a numbers game because there are millions of Chinese, Latin Americans, Asians, and white people who are not going to put up with this shit. I don't care about surviving, not me as an individual. If every black person in America were wiped out, the racists would only have a Pyrrhic victory. After the battle the racists would be so weakened that the enemies of this country could come in and pick the gold out of Rockefeller's teeth. We'd be glad to see that come about, because we want the world to be free, with or without us. There will be black people who will survive and continue to live. We survived everything else and we will survive Humphrey, Nixon, or Wallace.

The power structure could forestall this conflict. The politicians only have to start doing their duty; take a look at the oath of office that they have sworn to and start acting like people instead of demagogic pigs. Read the Constitution, the Bill of Rights, the Fourteenth Amendment. They want to know what we want. We want to take inventory of this country, everything in it, and we want our share. We want to share in everything, including the manipulation of America's destiny if we're going to be a part of it. If we can't have that, then we want out.

The Black Panther party is based on the black community—with those who have been unrepresented in the past, those who have been left out and alienated from all of the processes within this political system. The black people who are in Congress today are the representatives of the black middle class, in conjunction with the manipulators and exploiters of the white community. They are responsible for what we call community imperialism, whereby the black community is controlled from the sanctuary of the white community. They use the black middle class as puppets through whom they rule indirectly.

I'm opposed to all classes above the proletariat, of which I am a proud member. All the other classes are out of order and they're going to be abolished along with this system that spawns them. There are members of the black bourgeoisie who recognize that they have a responsibility to the people; they've abdicated the vested interests of the black middle class and they're coming back to the black people as a whole. We welcome their doing that.

Our differences with the black capitalists are the same as those with all the pigs in this country. We don't feel that capitalism is the solution to the problems of the black people. We need a Yankee-Doodle-Dandy version of socialism; we have to get away from the capitalistic system and start digging Karl Marx. He had a lot to say about how an economic system can be organized. We need a system that will be functional for the people, and it's not capitalism. It has to be a version of socialism, with the universal principles of socialism applied to this particular situation. I'm not saying we have to import the experience of the Russians, the Chinese, or the Cubans. If they've come up with any answers which would be helpful to us, we should have sense enough to use them without getting uptight. Why should we be ashamed or afraid to stand up and say that there is some information on hand that would improve the lives of all the people of the world?

Technologically speaking, productivity is such in this country, the means of production are so vast, that there's absolutely no reason for the people to be involved in a dog-eat-dog rat-race for existence. The reasons are political, not economic. This system is organized on a capitalistic basis so that in order for anything to happen, some big fat capitalist has to be able to make a profit or see some possibility of making a profit. I say that we need to put an end to the profit motive in civilization and substitute one of cooperation. Substitute the principle of cooperation, because there's no conflict on the face of the planet Earth today that cannot be solved. The war between the Arabs and the Jews—even that can be solved—they're all Semitic over there. If you get these capital-istic, imperialistic bastards out of Vietnam, if you get them out of the Middle East, and stop them from supplying arms to both sides, you can put an end to that conflict. Let them know that they're not going to be able to continue to steal oil from the Middle East, that the revenue from the oil should go to build up a life for the people there, and all the resources of the planet Earth should be employed to assure that every man, woman, and child receives the best standard of living human knowledge and technology can provide. They have a right to that, and anything and everything that stands in the way of that has got to go.

We have no need to fear taking a stand on this because, after all, the only thing they can do is put us in the penitentiary or kill us. That's the only choice they have, and the only choice they have as far as I'm concerned is killing me, because I'm not going back to the hole they call the penitentiary.

I can't begin to relate to the parole people who control those penitentiaries. I went there once on a field trip to investigate them so you wouldn't have to. I just want to say that there ain't nothing there. While I was there, I went through every part, from the hospital to solitary confinement. I didn't like anything about it, including the medicine, and they can have it. I'm not going back. I'd rather stay out here and die than go back in there and let those pigs have me up against the wall. I'm going to stay out here. Shoot me down in the streets. Shoot me right now. I'm not going back to the penitentiary.

I supposedly owe the penitentiary three years after being in-dicted by a county grand jury on the charge of assault with the intent to barbecue a pig. I appreciate them honoring me by giving me credit for that, but I'm sorry to say that I didn't have a gun. As a matter of fact, I got shot and went to the hospital. After the arrest, the judge released me on a writ of *habeas corpus* and charged the Department of Correction, the parole authorities, with persecuting me for political purposes. The prison officials didn't accept that, so they appealed his ruling to a higher three-pig court, which reversed the judge's decision and ordered me returned to prison. What they've done is destroyed or removed the presumption of innocence. Under this system of jurisprudence, all accused persons are presumed innocent until proven guilty—except parolees.

Those prisons are administered the way things are administered in the South—divide and rule. In the California prisons, you have three large ethnic groups: white, Mexican-American, and black. The pecking order is white first, Mexican-American second, and black last. The administrators have to balance-off tensions by pitting these groups against each other, because they have some common grievances and if those cats ever got together, they'd tear the walls down.

The prison people are racists from top to bottom. They get most of their guards from Mississippi and Alabama. They advertise down there in the post offices for people to come to California and get jobs as correctional officers.

I have no present plans for going to another country, either on business or as a fugitive from these pigs. I'm not going to run away and hide. I'm going to seek refuge in the black community, and I am going to depend upon members of the Black Panther party and other people in the community to see that I'm able to stay there without being molested by these pigs. I think it's time for people to stop running away from the problem, to stay here and confront it no matter what the cost.

Is it against the law to cuss in Washington, D.C.? Well, I didn't endorse that law, and I'm a taxpayer too. I get robbed for my money like everybody else, and I don't authorize a law against Eldridge Cleaver standing here and saying, "Fuck the pigs of the power structure!" I endorse the law that would permit that. So all of you misguided pigs who may be thinking of arresting me for that, I want you to know that as a member of the public and as one of your employers, I say, go somewhere else and watch all those Republicans and Democrats at their conventions where the crimes are being plotted and where you would be doing the most good.

I go around talking like this in public not because I have a five-

word vocabulary—I could straighten up on a few words—but because I know that it puts a lot of these chumps uptight, and I want
to keep them uptight in every way I can. If they don't like the way
I walk, I'm going to walk more like that. If they don't like the way
I talk, I'm going to talk more like that. That's why you young
people should let your hair grow long so they can freak out some
more. If there's anything we can do to put them uptight, let's do
it. Keep them uptight. Make them nervous until they have to stay
drunk in order to relate. Leave them and their alcoholic culture
because it's passé. It's out of style and nonfunctional for the present
and the future.

Of course, everything that we say might be wrong. We may be
committing crimes against nature. What we propose may be out-
rageous. I don't believe so, but we're not acquainted with any
ultimate truth. It may be that when we die, we will find ourselves
before the throne of God, looking up at Him with His long hippie
hair. He may pass a judgment on us and cast us down into the
hellfires to burn for days. We may find ourselves in hell burning
for what we said here today, and if we do, I'm going to look around
for you. Step forward when you see me coming down there and
we'll try to reactivate the Black Panther party, the Peace and
Freedom party, and move against the Devil, because we don't
have to accept him either. And if God comes down the elevator
in His asbestos suit and forms a coalition with the Devil to keep
us down there, we'll just have to move against Him too.

The people don't have to accept pain, oppression, and torture
from anything or anybody. Nobody is authorized to inflict pain,
torture, and suffering upon the people. And if we feel that way
about the Devil and God, then we definitely feel that way about
the pigs running around here and oinking in the faces of the people.

The sad part for them is that they're the ones with a crisis on
their hands, not us. The crisis is in their system, and meanwhile the
people are getting organized. They're coming together and they're
moving against the system, putting the pigs uptight. The pigs say
they're trying to save the situation for the people, and they are
frightening white people into believing that the victims of racism
have themselves become racists. The fact is that the orientation of

black people is totally counter to racism. They've been fighting racism ever since they got here. They don't want to practice it themselves, and they definitely don't want to continue being its victims. We oppose racism no matter what the color is—black, white, red, yellow, brown, blue, or green. We don't want it, we don't support it, and we're going to struggle against it; and we ask everybody to join in that struggle and let the people begin to write a history. Let there be a history of the people, for the people, and by the people. No more history of the pigs, for the pigs, and by the pigs. No more government of the pigs, for the pigs, and by the pigs.

Let's deal with this situation because the world demands it. What happens here in America decides the future of the entire world. We have madmen with their fingers on buttons that could destroy the world. The situation is too dangerous and the only hope for this country, the only hope for the world, is if the people get together and change the system as they have a right to do. They have a right to do it; they don't have to be intimidated by assassins, by court decrees, or by anything, because the spirit of the people is greater than the pigs' technology, whether the pigs know it or not.

They're not going to be able to heckle us or jeckle us and fuck us out of our rights as we see them. There are too many niggers in this country to go for that. If the white people want to play Nazis, we are not going to play Jews. We are going to defend ourselves and support each other. And we will join forces with those white people who join with us. Not only that, but we're going to join forces with all the revolutionary people of the world.

We call for the evacuation of the United States troops from Guantanamo Bay. Get the dagger out of the hearts of the Cuban people. We call for the immediate withdrawal of troops from Vietnam. Don't tell us that you have to go through all the negotiations in Paris. There ain't nothing to negotiate except our withdrawal. Get the pigs out of Vietnam and let the Vietnamese people enact their own destiny. It's their right and you don't have a right to be over there.

We want the boys to come back home because we know that

they're only over there because you've manipulated them with propaganda. You've told them they're doing their duty. You've told them that to be patriotic they have to answer the summons and go wherever General Hershey orders them to go. We want them to stop murdering the people over there. We want them back home, not to join the police force and murder us, but to join the people in forming a people's militia that would offer some defense for the people where they need it—right here against the pigs who want to turn America into another Nazi Germany.

That's what they're moving to do, and it's up to you to stop it because the fools like myself who stand up and run our mouths off, they're going to rip us off. They're going to lock us up, or they're going to shoot us down. The only thing that we ask is that you students "surprise us; it will be welcome provided that this, our battle cry, reach some receptive ear, that another hand reach out to pick up weapons, and that other fighting men come forward to intone our funeral dirge with the staccato of machine guns and new cries of battle and victory." [1]

All the power to the people! We need some student power and we need some faculty power, whether they want to give it or not. We need public servants who start acting like public servants and stop biting the hands that feed them—or the hand is going to have to rise up and slap that head off their shoulders, because we're not going to go for it anymore. All of you people who are in college, who are trying to decide which way to go, better make up your minds quick because they have pigs who will blow your mind for you, and I mean with a gun. Power!

[1] Quotation from Che Guevara—Eds.

APPENDIX

The University and Revolution course (33.490) was initiated at The American University in the fall of 1968 as a three-credit-hour independent-research course. During the academic year, 250 students were enrolled in the course and divided into seventeen sections—each section moderated by a faculty member who volunteered his services. Administrators and faculty received no pay for their participation.

The broad purpose of the course was to assess the impact of the university on the revolutionary movements sweeping the world today, as well as the impact of the revolutionary movements on the university. It was hoped that by reading, thinking about, and discussing these issues, students and professors would gain a better idea of what is happening in the world today and what would be appropriate responses. It was also hoped that the discipline of thought and rational reflection on student movements would help people to understand the historical causes, opportunities, and limitations of the movements.

Faculty members undertook specialized subtopics within this broad framework, which then became the subject of individual seminars: (1) The Black Student in the University and Revolution; (2) Individual Spiritual Awareness and Revolutionary Social Vision; (3) Effects of Social Revolution on the Structures and Functions of the Contemporary University; (4) The University and Revolution in the United States; (5) The University and Revolution: Philosophical Approaches; (6) The University and Revolution: A Radical Critique of the American Political System; (7) The University and Revolution: Latin America; (8) The University and Revolution: Southeast Asia; (9) The University and Revolution: France and Germany; (10) The Origin of Protest Movements at The American University; (11) What Is the Meaning of Due Process in the University?; (12) What Should Be Taught?

How Should It Be Taught?; (13) The University and Revolution: Socio-Psychological Approach.

Students attended general lectures and small seminars relating to the above topics. Most students received a pass or fail grade on an individual research project written in consultation with the seminar instructor. Some projects took two semesters to complete, giving students a total number of six credits.

The American University contributed $2,000 and the Student Association $2,500 to finance this course. This money was used to bring the following speakers to the campus: (1) Seymour M. Lipset, whose book *Student Politics* was used as a basic text for the course; (2) Jack Newfield, author of *A Prophetic Minority*; (3) Carl Oglesby, one of the founders of the Students for a Democratic Society (SDS); (4) Arthur Waskow of the Institute for Policy Studies; (5) Robert Theobald, British economist, cyberneticist, and author of *Dialogue* books on *Education* and *Youth* and *An Alternative Future for America*; (6) Eldridge Cleaver, author of *Soul on Ice*, 1968 Presidential candidate of the Peace and Freedom party, and Minister of Information, National Black Panther party; (7) Allard K. Lowenstein, past President of the National Student Association and U.S. Congressman from New York; (8) Russell Kirk, conservative educator and writer, author of *The Conservative Mind;* (9) Channing Phillips, Chairman of the Democratic Committee in the District of Columbia and Presidential nominee at the 1968 Democratic Convention; (10) Edmund Glenn, Professor of Intercultural Communication, University of Delaware; (11) Ewart Brown, leader of the Howard University student revolt in the spring of 1968; (12) Mark Rudd, leader of the Columbia University student revolt in the spring of 1968; (13) William F. Buckley, Jr., conservative intellectual, author, and editor of *National Review* magazine; (14) Paul Boutelle, Vice-Presidential candidate of the Socialist Workers' party; (15) Frank Wilkinson, Executive Chairman, National Committee to Abolish HUAC (House Un-American Activities Committee); (16) Robert Greenblatt, Co-chairman, National Mobilization Committee to End the War in Viet Nam; (17) Mike Spiegel, National Secretary, SDS; (18) Bernadine Dohran, legal counsel to SDS; (19) William Y. Elliott, University Professor,

The American University; author of *The Pragmatic Revolt in Politics*; (20) Glenn S. Dumke, historian and Chancellor, California State Colleges; (21) Sri Chinmoy, Indian spiritual teacher; (22) Ralph Abernathy, President, Southern Christian Leadership Conference (SCLC); (23) Dick Gregory, comedian, author, 1968 Presidential candidate of the Peace and Freedom party and "President-in-Exile"; (24) Nicholas von Hoffman, journalist and author of *We Are the People Our Parents Warned Us Against* and *Two, Three, Many More;* (25) Karl Dietrich-Wolff, President of the German Radical Student Movement.

NOTES ON THE CONTRIBUTORS

EWART BROWN, a native of Bermuda, served as Student Assembly President as an undergraduate of Howard University and was a principal leader in the 1967–68 undergraduate revolts at that school. He is presently the President of Howard Medical School's Freshman Class and led the 1969 student protests there.

ELDRIDGE CLEAVER is Minister of Information for the National Black Panther party and was the 1968 Presidential candidate of the Peace and Freedom party. Mr. Cleaver has spent most of his adult life in prison, where he wrote his best-selling book *Soul On Ice*. An anthology of his addresses to universities entitled *Elridge Cleaver: Post-Prison Writings and Speeches* has been published.

GLENN S. DUMKE is Chancellor of the California State Colleges, one of the largest systems of higher education in the western hemisphere. He is a former Chairman of the Membership and Standards Committee of the Western College Association and in 1967 was chosen as "Educator of the Year" by the Southern California Industry–Education Council. Dr. Dumke, a noted authority in Western American History, is the author of *The Boom of the Eighties in Southern California* and *Mexican Gold Trail*, and co-author of *A History of the Pacific Area in Modern Times*.

EDMUND S. GLENN, one of the foremost living semanticists, is Professor of Intercultural Communications at the University of Delaware and has served as the Chief of the Interpreting Branch of the Division of Language Services for the United States Department of State. He has been a personal interpreter for several United States Presidents and Secretaries of State. Dr. Glenn has been published widely in scientific and academic journals.

RUSSELL KIRK is one of the foremost conservative intellectuals in the United States, and has taught at several major universities. His syndicated column appears in over one hundred newspapers and in William Buckley's *National Review*. Dr. Kirk is author of such works as *The Conservative Mind, Academic Freedom,* and *The Intemperate Professor.*

SEYMOUR M. LIPSET is Professor of Government and Social Relations at Harvard University. He is also a Fellow of the Harvard Center for International Affairs and Director of the Comparative Universities Project, where he is currently engaged in a study of student activism and higher education in a cross-cultural perspective. Dr. Lipset is author of *Political Man* and *Revolution and Counterrevolution,* and has edited *Student Politics* (with Aldo Solari) and *Students and Politics* (with P. G. Altbach).

JACK NEWFIELD is a charter member of the Students for a Democratic Society and an assistant editor of *The Village Voice*. He is author of the widely acclaimed *A Prophetic Minority,* a probing study of the origins and development of the New Left.

MARK RUDD is one of the leaders of the Students for a Democratic Society. Mr. Rudd led the May 1968 student rebellion at Columbia University, which is of particular significance because it was one of the first true student takeovers of a major university in the United States. The tactics that Mr. Rudd and others developed have been used repeatedly in the campus unrest that has spread across the country.

SAMUEL L. SHARP, a native of Poland, is Professor of International Relations and Chairman of the Seminar on the Soviet Union and Eastern Europe in the Area Studies Programs in the School of International Service at The American University. Among his publications are *Poland: White Eagle in a Red Field, New Constitutions in the Soviet Sphere,* and *Nationalization of Key Industries in Eastern Europe.*

ROBERT THEOBALD is a British socioeconomist and cyberneticist who was born and raised in India. For the past ten years Mr. Theobald has worked primarily in the United States. His publications include: *The Rich and the Poor, Social Policies for America in the*

Seventies, Committed Spending, Dialogue on Youth, Dialogue on Violence, and *An Alternative Future for America.*

GARY R. WEAVER, co-editor of this volume, is an Instructor in the School of International Service at The American University. As former Assistant Dean in the School of International Service, he was co-founder of the course, University and Revolution, that inspired this volume.

JAMES H. WEAVER, co-editor of this volume, is the Chairman of the Economics Department at The American University and was former Chairman of the Faculty Senate at The American University. Dr. Weaver is also the co-founder of the University and Revolution course at The American University.

SELECTED BIBLIOGRAPHY

THE UNIVERSITY AND REVOLUTION: STRUCTURES AND FUNCTIONS

Books

Barzun, Jacques. *The American University: How It Runs, Where It Is Going.* New York: Harper & Row, Publishers, Inc., 1968.

Birenbaum, William M. *Overlive.* New York: Delacorte Press, Inc., 1969.

Editors of *Fortune. Youth in Turmoil.* New York: Time-Life Books, Inc., 1969.

Kerr, Clark. *The Uses of the University.* New York: Harper Torchbooks, 1963.

Lipset, Seymour M., ed. *Student Politics.* New York: Basic Books, Inc., 1967.

———, and Philip Altbach, eds. *Students and Politics.* Boston: Houghton Mifflin Company, 1969.

Long, Durward, Julian Foster, and Robert Gutchen, eds. *Students in Revolt.* New York: William Morrow & Co. Inc., 1969.

Martin, Warren B. *Alternatives to Irrelevance.* New York: Abingdon Press, 1968.

McCabe, John, ed. *Dialogues on Youth.* New York: The Bobbs-Merrill Company, Inc., 1967.

Ridgeway, James. *The Closed Corporation: American Universities in Crisis.* New York: Random House, Inc., 1968.

Riesman, David, and Christopher Jencks. *The Academic Revolution.* Garden City, New York: Doubleday & Company, Inc., 1968.

Schwab, Joseph J. *College Curriculum and Student Protest.* Chicago: The University of Chicago Press, 1969.

Theobald, Robert. *An Alternative Future for America.* Chicago: Swallow Press, 1968.

von Hoffman, Nicholas. *The Multiversity.* New York: Holt, Rinehart, and Winston, Inc., 1966.

Articles

"American Student Politics," *The American Scholar*, 36 (Autumn 1967), special issue.

Bettleheim, Bruno. "The Anatomy of Academic Discontent," *Change*, Vol. J, No. 3 (May–June 1969), pp. 18–27.

Feuer, Lewis S. "Should College Students Grade Their Teachers?" *New York Times* (September 18, 1966), pp. 56–60.

Keniston, Kenneth. "American Students and the 'Political Revival,'" *American Scholar*, 32 (Winter 1962–1963), pp. 40–65.

Rubin, Jerry. "Alliance for Liberation," *Liberation*, 11 (April 1966), pp. 9–12.

THE UNIVERSITY AND REVOLUTION: PHILOSOPHICAL APPROACHES

Books

Arendt, Hannah. *On Revolution*. New York: The Viking Press, Inc., 1963.

Booth, Wayne C., ed. *The Knowledge Most Worth Having*. Chicago: The University of Chicago Press, 1967.

Brinton, Crane. *The Anatomy of a Revolution*. New York: Random House, Inc., 1957.

Buckley, William F., Jr. *God and Man at Yale: The Superstition of Freedom*. Chicago: Henry Regnery Co., 1951.

Camus, Albert. *The Rebel*. New York: Alfred A. Knopf, Inc., 1954.

Debray, Regis. *Revolution in the Revolution*. New York: Grove Press, Inc., 1967.

Guevara, Ernesto. *Guerrilla War*. New York: Frederick A. Praeger, Inc., 1961.

Hoffer, Eric. *The Ordeal of Change*. New York: Harper & Row, Publishers, Inc., 1963.

Kesey, Ken. *One Flew Over the Cuckoo's Nest*. New York: Signet Books, 1962.

Mao Tse-tung. *On Guerrilla Warfare*. New York: Frederick A. Praeger, Inc., 1961.

Marcuse, Herbert. *An Essay on Liberation*. Boston: Beacon Press, 1969.
———. *Eros and Civilization*. Boston: Beacon Press, 1955.

————. *One-Dimensional Man*. Boston: Beacon Press, 1964.

Schwartz, Edward, ed. *Student Power, Philosophy, Program, Tactics*. Washington, D.C.: U.S. National Student Association, 1968.

Sibley, Mulford Q. *The Quiet Battle*. Boston: Beacon Press, 1963.

Swomley, John, Jr. *The Military Establishment*. Boston: Beacon Press, 1964.

Weinburg, Arthur and Lila. *Instead of Violence*. Boston: Beacon Press, 1965.

Wolff, Robert Paul. *The Poverty of Liberalism*. Boston: Beacon Press, 1968.

Articles

Altbach, Philip G. "The Future of the American Student Movement," *Liberal Education*, 52 (October 1966), pp. 313–24.

Brogan, D. W. "The Student Revolt," *Encounter*, 31 (July 1968), pp. 20–25.

Chomsky, Noam. "The Responsibility of Intellectuals," *New York Review of Books* (February 23, 1967), pp. 16–26.

Goodman, Paul. "Freedom and Learning: The Need for Choice," *Saturday Review* (May 18, 1968), pp. 73–75.

Moynihan, Daniel P. "Nirvana Now," *The American Scholar*, Vol. 36, No. 4 (Autumn 1967), 539–48.

THE UNIVERSITY AND REVOLUTION: SOCIO-PSYCHOLOGICAL APPROACHES

Books

Erikson, Erik. *Childhood and Society*. New York: W. W. Norton & Company, Inc., 1963.

————. *Identity: Youth and Crisis*. New York: W. W. Norton and Company, Inc., 1968.

————, ed. *The Challenge of Youth*. Garden City, New York: Doubleday & Company, Inc., 1965.

————. *Young Man Luther*. New York: W. W. Norton & Company, Inc., 1958.

Goodman, Paul. *Growing Up Absurd: Problems of Youth in the Organized System.* New York: Random House, Inc., 1960.

Hoffer, Eric. *The True Believer.* New York: Harper & Row, Publishers, Inc., 1951.

Keniston, Kenneth. *The Uncommitted: Alienated Youth in American Society.* New York: Harcourt, Brace and World, 1965.

————. *The Young Radicals: Notes on Committed Youth.* New York: Harcourt, Brace & World, Inc., 1968.

Lindner, Robert. *Must You Conform?* New York: Grove Press, Inc., 1961.

Moore, Barrington. *The Social Organs of Dictatorship and Democracy.* Boston: Beacon Press, 1966.

Sanford, Nevitt. *Where Colleges Fail: A Study of the Student as a Person.* San Francisco: Jossey-Bass, 1967.

Journals

Journal of Social Issues, 1945– .

Articles

Flacks, Richard. "The Liberated Generation: An Exploration of Rules of Student Protest," *Journal of Social Issues,* 23 (July 1967), pp. 52–75.

Keniston, Kenneth. "Youth, Change, and Violence," *The American Scholar,* (Spring 1968), pp. 227–45.

————. "You Have to Grow Up in Scarsdale to Know How Bad Things Really Are," *New York Times Magazine* (April 27, 1969).

Kolden, Rolf. "Growing Up Revoluting," *The Activist* (Fall 1967).

Riesman, David. "The Uncommitted Generation," *Encounter,* 15 (November 1966), pp. 25–30.

THE NEW LEFT: CAMPUS REVOLTS

Books

Cohen, Mitchell and Dennis Hale, eds. *The Student Left: An Anthology.* Boston: Beacon Press, 1966.

Davidson, Carl. *The New Radicals in the Multiversity.* Chicago: Students for a Democratic Society, 1968.

Draper, Hal. *Berkeley: The New Student Revolt.* New York: Grove Press, Inc., 1965.

Editors of *The Atlantic Monthly. The Troubled Campus.* Boston: Little, Brown and Company, 1966.

Howe, Irving, ed. *Student Activism.* Indianapolis: The Bobbs-Merrill Company, Inc., 1967.

Jacobs, Paul and Saul Landau. *The New Radicals.* New York: Vintage Books, 1966.

Kunen, James S. *The Strawberry Statement: Notes of a College Revolutionary.* New York: Random House, Inc., 1969.

Luce, Philip Abbott. *The New Left.* New York: David McKay Co., Inc., 1966.

Mailer, Norman. *Miami and the Siege of Chicago: An Informal History of the Republican and Democratic Conventions of 1968.* New York: Signet Books, 1968.

Newfield, Jack. *A Prophetic Minority.* New York: The New American Library, 1966.

Rader, Dotson. *I Ain't Marchin' Anymore!* New York: David McKay Co., Inc., 1969.

Students for a Democratic Society. *The Port Huron Statement.* New York: Students for a Democratic Society, 1964.

von Hoffman, Nicholas. *Two, Three, Many More.* New York: Quadrangle Books, 1969.

————. *We Are the People Our Parents Warned Us Against.* Chicago: Quadrangle Books, 1968.

Walker, Daniel. *Rights in Conflict.* New York: E. P. Dutton & Co., Inc., 1968.

Young, Alfred F., ed. *Dissent: Explorations in the History of American Radicalism.* DeKalb, Ill.: Northern Illinois University Press, 1968.

Journals

Activist (student-edited moderate-left quarterly), 1961– .

New Left Notes (weekly paper of the Students for a Democratic Society), 1966– .

"Students and Politics," *Daedalus: Journal of the American Academy of Arts and Sciences,* Vol. 97, No. 1 (Winter 1968).

"Stirrings Out of Apathy: Student Activism and the Decade of Protest," *Journal of Social Issues,* Vol. XXIII, No. 3 (July 1967).

The New Student Left (bibliography). The Free Society Association, 1965.

Articles

Aptheker, Herbert. "The Academic Rebellion in the U.S.," *Political Affairs,* 44 (August 1965), pp. 34–41.

Crane, Robert M. "Unrest on Campus—Revolution or Evolution?" *College and University,* 42 (Winter 1967), pp. 209–17.

Farber, Jerry. "The Student as Nigger," *This Magazine Is About Schools,* 2 (Winter 1968), pp. 107–16.

Goodman, Paul. "The New Aristocrats," *Playboy,* 14 (March 1967), pp. 110–11, 152–59.

Halsendulph, Ernest and John Matthews. "When Students Take Over a Campus," *New Republic* (April 13, 1968), p. 10.

Hayden, Tom. "Just a Matter of Timing?" *Liberation,* 7 (October 1962), pp. 24–26.

———. "The Ability to Face What Comes," *New Republic,* 154 (January 15, 1966), pp. 16–18.

Kirk, Russell. "Politically Ignorant College Students; Recrudescent Communist Movement on the Campus," *National Review,* 17 (May 18, 1965), p. 423.

Luce, Philip Abbott. "Why I Quit the Extreme Left," *Saturday Evening Post* (May 8, 1965), pp. 32–33.

Newfield, Jack. "Real Revolt on Campus," *Commonweal,* 75 (December 15, 1961), pp. 309–11.

———. "Revolt Without Dogma," *Motive,* 26 (October 1965), pp. 20–24.

———. "The Student Left: Idealism and Action," *Nation,* 201 (November 8, 1965), pp. 330–33.

Waskow, Arthur. "The New Student Movement," *Our Generation,* 3 (May 1966), pp. 52–54.

THE UNIVERSITY AND REVOLUTION:
THE BLACK REVOLUTION

Books

Brown, Claude. *Manchild in the Promised Land.* New York: The Macmillan Company, 1965.

Carmichael, Stokely and Charles Hamilton. *Black Power.* New York: Random House, Inc., 1967.

Cleaver, Eldridge. *Soul On Ice.* New York: McGraw-Hill Book Company, 1968.

————. (Ed. Robert Scheer). *Eldridge Cleaver: Post-Prison Writings and Speeches.* New York: Random House, Inc., 1969.

Cobbs, Price M. and William H. Grier. *Black Rage.* New York: Basic Books, Inc., 1968.

Fanon, Frantz. *The Wretched of the Earth.* New York: Grove Press, Inc., 1965.

Gregory, Dick. *The Shadow That Scares Me.* New York: Pocket Books, Inc., 1968.

Hersey, John. *The Algiers Motel Incident.* New York: Alfred A. Knopf, Inc., 1968.

Kardiner, Abram and Lionel Ovesey. *The Mark of Oppression: Explorations in the Personality of the American Negro.* Cleveland: World Publishing Company, 1962.

Lester, Julius. *Look Out Whitey, Black Power's Gon' Get Your Mama.* New York: The Dial Press, Inc., 1968.

Malcolm X. *The Autobiography of Malcolm X.* New York: Grove Press, Inc., 1964.

Nelson, Truman. *The Right of Revolution.* Boston: Beacon Press, 1968.

Report of the National Advisory Commission on Civil Disorders. New York: E. P. Dutton & Co., Inc., 1968.

Savio, Mario, et al. *The Free Speech Movement and the Negro Revolution.* Detroit: News and Letters, 1965.

Willis, Gary. *The Second Civil War: Arming for Armageddon.* New York: Signet Books, 1968.

Zinn, Howard. *SNCC: The New Abolitionists.* Boston: Beacon Press, 1964.

Journals

The Movement (Publication of the Student Non-Violent Coordinating Committee of California), 1965– .

Articles

Hayden, Tom. "SNCC: The Qualities of Protest," *Studies on the Left*, 5 (Winter 1965), pp. 113–24.

Newfield, Jack. "The Question of SNCC," *Nation*, 201 (July 19, 1965), pp. 37–40.